S. Hrg. 113–214

CARCIERI: BRINGING CERTAINTY TO TRUST LAND ACQUISITIONS

HEARING

BEFORE THE

COMMITTEE ON INDIAN AFFAIRS
UNITED STATES SENATE

ONE HUNDRED THIRTEENTH CONGRESS

FIRST SESSION

NOVEMBER 20, 2013

Printed for the use of the Committee on Indian Affairs

U.S. GOVERNMENT PRINTING OFFICE

87–133 PDF   WASHINGTON : 2014

For sale by the Superintendent of Documents, U.S. Government Printing Office
Internet: bookstore.gpo.gov   Phone: toll free (866) 512–1800; DC area (202) 512–1800
Fax: (202) 512–2104   Mail: Stop IDCC, Washington, DC 20402–0001

CONTENTS

CARCIERI: BRINGING CERTAINTY TO TRUST LAND ACQUISITIONS

WEDNESDAY, NOVEMBER 20, 2013

U.S. SENATE,
COMMITTEE ON INDIAN AFFAIRS,
Washington, DC.

The Committee met, pursuant to notice, at 2:30 p.m. in room 628, Dirksen Senate Office Building, Hon. Maria Cantwell, Chairman of the Committee, presiding.

OPENING STATEMENT OF HON. MARIA CANTWELL, U.S. SENATOR FROM WASHINGTON

The CHAIRWOMAN. The Senate Indian Affairs Committee will come to order.

Welcome to all. We are having an oversight hearing tody to receive testimony on *Carcieri*: Bringing Certainty to Trust Land Acquisitions. And I know the Vice Chairman of the Committee will be here shortly.

We have a busy agenda today, so I want to go ahead and get started with my opening statement and then to welcome our colleague, Senator Feinstein from California, who is also with us here today and will be part of our first discussion, followed by the Honorable Kevin Washburn. And then a panel of leaders to discuss their views on this issue.

This afternoon, the Committee is holding an oversight hearing on *Carcieri*, as I said, in an attempt to bring certainty to trust land acquisitions. Since the earliest days of our republic, the United States and tribes have had a government-to-government relationship that is based on treaties and agreements. The fundamental element of these agreements is that tribes secured lands that would be their homelands and territories. The government-to-government relationship continued, but not before some measures were tried to forcibly assimilate Native American people. But Congress passed the Indian Reorganization Act of 1934 to say that those policies were a disaster.

So for the period of 1887 to 1933, approximately 90 million acres of tribal land went out of tribal ownership. By 1934, the then-Commissioner of Indian Affairs, John Collier, stated that tribal lands had been diminished by 80 percent, and the value of tribal lands had decreased 85 percent.

So when Congress enacted the Indian Reorganization Act of 1934, it represented a fundamental shift away from the United States' failed policies of the 19th century. America returned to recognizing tribes as a government, and dealing with them in a government-to-government relationship with shared goals of strengthening tribal communities and improving the lives of Native Americans.

The purpose of the Indian Reorganization Act was three-fold. One, to halt Federal polices of allotment and assimilation; to reverse the negative impacts of allotment policies; and three, to secure for all tribes a base of trust land to engage in economic development and self-determination. The bill aimed to restore tribal land bases by stopping the loss of more lands and allowing consolidation of existing land and acquiring new land, all of which was then placed into trust.

Since 1934, the United States has taken approximately 10 million acres of land into trust on behalf of tribes. As Chair, I will note that I think less than 1 percent of that land has been used for gaming.

Since the enactment of the Indian Reorganization Act, tribal governments have flourished, and tribes have adopted constitutions and created governmental departments and have been better able to serve their people and protect their rights. It has also enabled a cultural revitalization within Indian people, being more free to practice their traditions. These were the goals of the Indian Reorganization Act, and they remain relevant today as many tribes do not have any land or sufficient land to meet the needs of their people.

In 1994, Congress made an adjustment to the Indian Reorganization Act. Because the Department of Interior began to treat treaties differently, based on whether they were federally recognized. Our late colleague, Senator Inouye, led the effort in 1994 to amend the Indian Reorganization Act to ensure that all federally recognized tribes are treated equally, including the right to have land taken into trust.

But we are at a crossroads again, almost 20 years later, and now we must reaffirm Congressional intent to take land into trust for all tribes under the Indian Reorganization Act. The Indian Gaming Act and the provisions that allowed tribes to game on off-reservation land have made the land into trust process more visible and, in some cases, more complex. Of the 10 million acres that have been taken into trust since 1934, as I said, only a very small amount has been for gaming. This is clear from a recent report by the Interior Department. The last five years, most of the trust land applications have been for agriculture development, energy infrastructure and housing.

So these are the very reasons that Congress sought the Indian Reorganization Act, to ensure the tribes would have these kinds of controls. So almost 20 years after Congress clarified that all tribes should be treated equally, we are here again today because a Supreme Court decision in 2009, *Carcieri v. Salazar*, has once again created two classes of tribes. The Supreme Court narrowly defined the tribes that could have taken land into trust as only those tribes under Federal jurisdiction in 1934. This decision reversed what had been 80 years of Federal policy to restore land holdings and strengthen tribal governments.

The Supreme Court's decision did two things that greatly undermined the Federal relationship with tribes and the Federal policy to support tribal self-governance. First, the decision created two classes of tribes: tribes that can legally take land into trust and tribes that can't. This is contrary to the fundamental principle of creating equality of Native Americans in this particular area.

Secondly, the Supreme Court decision resulted in a chilling effect for tribes in all of land into trust issues. It has created a great deal of uncertainty as tribes try to move forward within their communities on economic development efforts. Since the court's decision, tribal organizations and other stakeholders have asked this Committee to bring back certainty into the process. The impacts of *Carcieri* have been felt throughout Indian Country and have resulted in the loss of economic opportunity, stalled a lot of infrastructure projects and increased litigation and bureaucratic delays at the Department of Interior.

In addition to the *Carcieri* decision, the Supreme Court's recent decision on *Patchak* also has held a challenge to the land into trust decisions and this is something we will be hearing about today as well.

If the *Carcieri* decision is left to stand, the result will be the perpetration of two classes of tribes. This is inconsistent with the Indian Reorganization Act and this is why we must bring certainty back into the process today.

I want to make sure one thing is clear. The government-to-government relationship between tribal governments and the Federal Government must be preserved. We are seeking certainty and clarity in the land into trust process. But it cannot be at the expense of tribal sovereignty, and not in a way that impacts that trust relationship.

So we will be hearing today from a variety of people to bring light to this issue and hopefully be able to move forward and resolve this issue once and for all.

I again appreciate everyone's attention and the witnesses who are here today. Now I would like to turn to the Vice Chairman for his statement on this.

STATEMENT OF HON. JOHN BARRASSO, U.S. SENATOR FROM WYOMING

Senator BARRASSO. Thank you, Madam Chairman, for holding this hearing. To start off, I welcome our friend and our colleague, Senator Feinstein, to the hearing. I know she is very busy, so I am going to be brief.

This Committee has held several hearings in the past two Congresses examining the impacts of the Supreme Court case, *Carcieri v. Salazar*, the impact on tribes and their lands. The Committee has also examined and passed legislation in the past two Congresses regarding this case. I know you have worked diligently to find a resolution to this difficult case, and I hope to hear from our witnesses today on how to move forward on this matter.

Thank you, and thank you all for being here today. Thank you, Madam Chairwoman.

The CHAIRWOMAN. Thank you, Senator Barrasso. Does my colleague from Alaska have an opening statement?

Senator BEGICH. Madam Chair, if I can wait until after Senator Feinstein, given her time, but I do have a couple quick comments before the next panel, if that is okay.

The CHAIRWOMAN. Okay, thank you.

Senator Feinstein, the floor is yours. Thank you so much for working with our Committee on this issue, and thank you for being here before the Committee today.

STATEMENT OF HON. DIANNE FEINSTEIN, U.S. SENATOR FROM CALIFORNIA

Senator FEINSTEIN. I thank you as well, Madam Chairman, and Dr. Barrasso and Senator Begich, thank you also for being here.

Let me just begin by thanking you for your willingness to hear from local governments as well as tribes, to get the full picture of how the fee to trust process affects communities across the Nation. I want to particularly thank you for inviting supervisor Diane Dillon from Napa County, California. She is directly behind me. Supervisor Dillon is experiencing first-hand the challenges that go along with recognition and trust land acquisition. So I know she will speak with some authority about the difficulties that face local governments.

As you may be aware, there are more than 100 federally recognized tribes in California. There are likely to be many more that will seek recognition in the near future. But what really sets California apart is the scale of the tribal gaming industry. According to the American Gaming Association, there are 70 tribal gaming establishments in the State today. All of these facilities have opened in the last 15 years.

As of 2010, the total revenue of these gaming establishments was valued at $6.78 billion, more than twice that of any other State. By that measure, it is approaching the size of the gaming industry in Nevada, which is valued at just over $10 billion. My concern is that California tribes, some of them, are no longer content with casinos on Indian lands, despite the fact that they agreed in a State-wide ballot measure in 2000, called Proposition 1A, that tribal gaming would be confined to Indian lands.

In recent years, we have seen the number of reservation shopping proposals increase. These are proposals that are in direct conflict with Proposition 1A. A landless tribe from Santa Cruz tried to open a casino near Oakland. Another landless tribe from Mendocino tried to do the same just miles down the road from Oakland in Richmond, California. A tribe that has a reservation in Butte County convinced the Secretary of the Interior to approve a casino 50 miles away in Yuba County near Sacramento. And a tribe with land in the Sierra foothills convinced the Secretary to approve a casino outside Fresno, more than 40 miles away.

Now, this issue is not limited to California. It is in Wisconsin, there is a fight in Arizona, it is in Michigan, it is in Oregon and it is in Washington. My full statement, which goes into the record, will describe each situation.

The purpose of these moves is clear. Tribes want to open casinos near major urban areas to increase their profits. And the effect of major off-reservation casinos I think is undeniable. Large casinos require local resources, including increased costs for police, fire, water, sewer and transportation.

But here is the catch. When new trust lands are acquired, tribes are under no obligation to mitigate these impacts. The Department of Interior also has no obligation to address local concerns.

I strongly believe that local governments must have the ability to influence the terms and conditions of the development of new casinos, especially because many communities simply do not want new casinos in their back yard. These casinos are not small. They are done by syndicates out of Atlantic City, out of Las Vegas, out of New Jersey.

Take the case of Butte County. When the tribe from Butte County proposed a casino in Yuba County, Yuba County voters were so opposed to the casino that they put an advisory measure on the ballot. The voters rejected the proposed casino. But the Department of Interior ignored the voters and approved the tribe's request for the casino. I don't think this should be allowed to happen.

I understand the intent of the *Carcieri* fix. And I do not accept the notion that tribes recognized before the 1934 Indian Reorganization Act have more rights than their counterparts that were recognized after 1934. But any *Carcieri* fix must in my view and the view of some others address concerns about tribal gaming. I do believe there is room to work with your Committee, Madam Chairman, to hopefully find common ground on a path forward.

One way to fix the problem would be to enact the Tribal Gaming Eligibility Act, a bill I introduced with Senator Roberts earlier this year. The bill takes critical, common-sense steps to slow reservation shopping and to protect those communities that are opposed to new casino developments by requiring tribes to demonstrate both a modern and an aboriginal connection to the land before opening new gaming establishments. As it is now, a tribe can buy a mall somewhere in a community, shut it down and open a gaming establishment.

Other reforms that could be part of the solution include prohibiting land taken into trust for non-gaming purposes from being used for casinos at a later date, requiring tribes to mitigate jurisdictional conflicts and effects as a condition of trust acquisitions, increasing notice and comment periods for local governments, and requiring the Department of the Interior to consider that input, which they largely do not. Collectively, these reforms would help address some of my concerns.

When combined with the requirement that tribes demonstrate modern and aboriginal ties to the land, these reforms would in my view represent a real improvement in the fee to trust process.

Let me just say one other thing that has concerned me. With 70 big gaming institutions, IGRA has a very minor regulatory and supervisory role. Las Vegas gaming has hundreds of regulators and supervisors. And long term, I think this presents a problem. Because casinos have their own problems with skimming, with other irregular activities and sometimes criminal activities. I think you have found that, it is Las Vegas' history, it is Atlantic City's history and so on.

We would like to work with you. In my view, the fact that the Indian tribes of California went to the ballot, they told the people one thing, and that is that the Indian gaming would be on tribal land, and in fact now, there is effort after effort to move away from that concept is candidly unacceptable. Because you reach a point where with 70 operating casinos, enough is enough.

So I thank you very much for listening. This has been my point of view. And I might say that there is growing concern in California. I think Supervisor Dillon will point out where there is a tribe that now wants to put a gaming casino right in the middle of Napa Valley. And there is one reason, and that is a problem.

So in any event, welcome to the conflict, and I thank you for your courtesy.

[The prepared statement of Senator Feinstein follows:]

PREPARED STATEMENT OF HON. DIANNE FEINSTEIN, U.S. SENATOR FROM CALIFORNIA

Madam Chairwoman, Mr. Ranking Member, thank you for the opportunity to testify.

I appreciate your willingness to hear from local governments as well as tribes to get the *full picture* of how the fee-to-trust process affects communities across the nation.

I want to particularly thank you for inviting Supervisor Diane Dillon from Napa County, California. Supervisor Dillon is experiencing firsthand the challenges that go along with the recognition and trust land acquisition process. So I know she will speak with great authority about the difficulties that face local governments.

As you may be aware, there are more than 100 federally recognized tribes in California. And there are likely to be many more that will seek recognition in the near future.

But what really sets California apart is the scale of the tribal gaming industry.

- According to the American Gaming Association, there are 70 tribal gaming establishments in the state today. *All of these facilities have opened in the last 15 years*;
- As of 2010, *the total revenue of these gaming establishments was valued at $6.78 billion*, more than twice that of any other state.
- By that measure, it is approaching the size of the gaming industry in Nevada, which is valued at just over $10 billion.

My concern is that California tribes are no longer content with casinos on Indian lands, despite the fact that they agreed in a state ballot measure in 2000 ("Proposition 1A") that tribal gaming would be confined to Indian lands.

In recent years we have seen the number of reservation shopping proposals increase. These are proposals that are in direct conflict with Proposition 1A.

- A landless tribe from Santa Cruz tried to open a casino near Oakland.
- Another landless tribe from Mendocino tried to do the same, just miles down the road from Oakland in Richmond, California.
- A tribe that has a reservation in Butte County convinced the Secretary of the Interior to approve a casino nearly 50 miles away in Yuba County, near Sacramento.
- And a tribe with land in the Sierra foothills convinced the secretary to approve a casino outside Fresno, more than 40 miles away.

This issue is not limited to California.

- In Wisconsin, the Menominee (Mih-NOM-min-nee) tribe received approval for a casino almost 200 miles from the tribe's reservation.
- The City of Glendale, Arizona, is disputing the Tohono O'odham (Toe-hoe-no OH-tham) Nation's proposal to open a casino and resort in the city's urban sport and entertainment district, which even by the tribe's own admission is at least 75 miles from its reservation's border.
- The Little River Band of Ottawa Indians has proposed to build a casino in Fruitport Township, Michigan, approximately 90 miles south of the tribe's headquarters.

- In Oregon, the Coquille (Ko-Kwell) Indian Tribe has been purchasing land in the Interstate 5 corridor near Medford, approximately 160 miles southeast of the tribe's land.
- And as you are aware, Madam Chairwoman, the Spokane Tribe of Indians in Washington is proposing to build an off-reservation casino.

The purpose of these moves is clear-tribes want to open casinos near major urban areas to increase their profits.

The effect of major off-reservation casinos is undeniable.

Large casinos require local resources, including increased costs for police, fire, water, sewer and transportation.

But here's the catch: when new trust lands are acquired, tribes are under no obligation to mitigate these impacts. That Department of the Interior also has no obligation to address local concerns.

I strongly believe that local governments must have the ability to influence the terms and conditions of the development of new casinos, especially because many communities simply do not want new casinos in their backyard.

Take the case of the tribe from Butte County, California. When the tribe from Butte County proposed a casino in Yuba County, Yuba County voters were so opposed to the casino proposal that they put an advisory measure on the ballot. Voters rejected the proposed casino. *But the Department of the Interior ignored the voters and approved the tribe's request for a casino.* This should not be allowed to happen.

I understand the intent of the *Carcieri* Fix. And I do not accept the notion that tribes recognized *before* the 1934 Indian Reorganization Act have more rights than their counterparts that were recognized *after* 1934.

But any *Carcieri* fix must address concerns about tribal gaming.

I do believe there is room to work with the Committee to find common ground on a path forward.

One way to fix the problem would be to enact the Tribal Gaming Eligibility Act, a bill I introduced with Senator Roberts earlier this year. The bill takes critical, common-sense steps to slow reservation shopping, and to protect those communities that are opposed to new casino developments, by requiring tribes to demonstrate both a modern and an aboriginal connection to the land before *opening new gaming establishments.*

Other reforms that could be a part of the solution include:

- Prohibiting land taken into trust for non-gaming purposes from being used for casinos at a later date.
- Requiring tribes to mitigate jurisdictional conflicts and effects as a condition for trust acquisitions,
- Increasing notice and comment periods for local governments, and requiring the Department of the Interior to consider that input.

Collectively, these reforms would help address some of my concerns.

When combined with the requirement that tribes demonstrate modern and aboriginal ties to the land, I believe these reforms would represent a real improvement in the fee to trust process.

Thank you again for this opportunity, Madam Chairwoman.

I hope to continue working with you and this committee to solve these issues and I hope we will pass a *Carcieri* fix soon.

The CHAIRWOMAN. Thank you, Senator Feinstein. Thank you for being here today and for your testimony. I know this is an issue you have been following for some time, and we appreciate your due diligence here. We will look forward to, after today's witnesses, dialoguing with you more.

Unless my colleagues have any questions for our colleague? Thank you.

Senator Begich?

STATEMENT OF HON. MARK BEGICH, U.S. SENATOR FROM ALASKA

Senator BEGICH. Thank you, Madam Chair, and thank you for holding this hearing. I know Assistant Secretary Washburn is going to be up next, and I look forward to seeing him again.

In my opinion, from an Alaska context on this, the legislative fix of the 2009 Supreme Court ruling regarding the ability for tribes to take land in trust, this is not a place, and I know there is some work here, this is not a place to solve or deal with Alaska issues, which are very different. Hearing about all the gaming, we have no gaming in Alaska, so it is a non-issue for us.

But I want to make it very clear that we have many issues to deal with in Alaska, and this is not, for us, a place to deal with it within the *Carcieri* fix.

But let me also say that there were some rulings this last summer through the D.C. District Court that the State of Alaska and the Secretary are in arguments now with Alaska tribe regarding this issue and are going through the court process. So again, I would make the point very clearly here that we do not want to use, from purely Alaska's perspective, this legislation to do anything to offset what is moving forward. We think it is a good settlement and a good opportunity.

I also want to say that I am anxious to see what the House does and produces. I know there have been discussions here on the Senate side for what we are going to do. My understanding is, the status quo for Alaska will be there, which I appreciate. Again, I don't want to have anything in this legislation that changes the way Alaska has been operating. I don't want any Alaska provisions in there, again, because we are moving through the court system. We have our own track we are dealing with, many other issue to focus on.

I am anxious to get this done. I think ever since I got here, to be frank with you, Madam Chair, I did not know much about this until within about one month of getting here. Then suddenly it was one after another who was talking to me about this issue. It is clear to me that there has to be a legislative fix. I am anxious to work through that, anxious to deal with this issue once and for all. I think there are good arguments I have heard from a lot of tribes regarding the issue of putting land into trust.

We are unique in Alaska. We don't have that situation. We do have one tribe that is now going, as I said, through the court process on this issue. So I am anxious to work with the Committee, do whatever I can to move this legislation forward. But I want to make it very clear here that we are not interested, from my perspective as an Alaskan, representing Alaska tribes, which is about 230 plus tribes, interested in putting anything in this bill that changes the way it is today. I think there are so many tribes in the lower 48 that have to get this resolved one way or another. So I am anxious to move this forward in whatever way we can.

Thank you for having this hearing. I will have some questions for the Assistant Secretary, and thank you for doing this.

The CHAIRWOMAN. Thank you.

I want to turn back to the Vice Chairman, Senator Barrasso.

Senator BARRASSO. Thank you very much, Madam Chairwoman

Just a second thought. Earlier today there was a Congressional Gold Medal Ceremony in honor of Native American Code Talkers. A number of members of this Committee were in attendance, obviously bipartisan. Senator Johnson had a chance to speak and tell some of the history I just think this Committee meeting the same day, perhaps there are some here in attendance who were able to attend this marvelous ceremony in Emancipation Hall to thank those who made such incredible sacrifices, true heroes as Code Talkers, and a story that for a long time wasn't told intentionally because people were told to be quiet when they went home from the war. Many times their families weren't even aware of the incredible sacrifices.

But you talk about effectiveness, and true heroes of World War II. So just as we meet today in this Committee hearing, I thought it would be good for the record to recognize this Congressional Gold Medal ceremony today in honor of our Native American Code Talkers.

Thank you, Madam Chair.

The CHAIRWOMAN. Thank you very much for bringing that up. It was a very beautiful ceremony, and great participation and recognition for individuals who played such an incredible role for our Country.

I want to note our former colleague and Chair of this Committee, the late Senator Inouye, was also honored today with the Medal of Freedom. His work was being recognized at the White House. So many of us participated last night in a reception to remember him and his work on this Committee. We want to also remember his great contribution. So thank you for doing that.

We will next turn back to our hearing and our panel today. We are going to start with Assistant Secretary Kevin Washburn. Thank you for being with us again today, and your hard work on this issue.

STATEMENT OF HON. KEVIN WASHBURN, ASSISTANT SECRETARY—INDIAN AFFAIRS, U.S. DEPARTMENT OF THE INTERIOR

Mr. WASHBURN. Thank you, Madam Chair, Mr. Vice Chairman and Senator Begich. It is good to be back here. I feel like I never left.

I am here today to thank you for your leadership on the *Carcieri* issue, and for doing the hard work of trying to find a way forward to mitigate the harmful effects of this decision. We have testified on numerous occasions on this subject, and we continue to support your efforts to achieve a *Carcieri* fix. Since we have testified so often before, I will be brief, rather than repeating the same testimony.

I would note that the last week, last Wednesday, President Obama himself reaffirmed the Administration's commitment to a *Carcieri* fix. We had the White House Tribal Nations conference, and the President was there, and the 13 Cabinet secretaries, and Senator Begich, too. We were glad to see him there, thank you, Senator. And he made a point of doing so from the podium, the President did, asked for a *Carcieri* fix.

Some people suggest that we need to use this as an opportunity to consider broader issues of land into trust. They also suggest that we give tribes sort of a careful questioning about what they are going to use the land for. I kind of want to push back against that. We do inquire what the purpose of the land into trust application is routinely. We always do that.

That is how we know, for example, that the largest number of land into trust applications is for agriculture. The second most is for infrastructure, such as health care facilities, schools and police stations and those sorts of things. Third, for economic development, but not including gaming. And fourth, for housing. Of the nearly 1,500 acquisitions since the beginning of 2009 that we have made, fewer than 20 have been for gaming. So gaming is really the small exception that ends up having a great deal of public attention, but it does not represent the heartland of land into trust in any way.

And I frankly sometimes wonder why we ask tribes at all what the purpose is for taking land into trust. If you ask most Americans why do they want a home, they look at you like you are crazy. It is not something you need to explain. People have a reason in their heart, and it is more than just shelter. It is something deep within the American psyche. I think you find people hard pressed to explain it. It is hard to put into words.

We characterize, indeed, home ownership as the American dream. And families need homes to thrive. It is not different for Indian tribes. What we are doing here is trying to ensure that tribes have home lands, so tribes can thrive as well. But their homelands were taken, as Senator Cantwell very eloquently stated in her opening statement. A lot of acres, millions of acres were taken from tribes. So their American dream is a little more cloudy than it is for the rest of America.

At the time, at the end of the allotment era, Congress made a decision that we were going to stop eviscerating the tribal land mass, and we were going to try to restore it. So Congress made that decision, and that decision has been made for many decades now. The Obama Administration has been very, very committed to it, as everybody well knows.

The fact is though that some tribes may be denied the American dream by the *Carcieri* decision. So this is a very important issue.

Some people may think that I am taking liberties to compare tribal governments to Americans and their dream for a home. But I think that analogy is apt. But if you prefer just to talk about the governmental analogy, we also don't quiz western cities or counties very hard when they say they want to expand into unincorporated areas. If you ask a county why it is going to do that, it is going to say because it wants to take care of its community. That is a common feeling.

Tribal governments are no different. There are a myriad of reasons why they take land into trust, but the bottom line is that they want homelands and they want to be able to provide for their people. In America, this is a good enough reason to take land into trust.

I think this is one of the most important issues of our time in Indian Country. The question is whether we are going to deny some tribes homelands or the ability to expand their homelands, while others have that ability. So again, I want to thank the Committee for bringing attention to this extremely important issue, and I stand ready for questions.

[The prepared statement of Mr. Washburn follows:]

PREPARED STATEMENT OF HON. KEVIN WASHBURN, ASSISTANT SECRETARY—INDIAN AFFAIRS, U.S. DEPARTMENT OF THE INTERIOR

I. Introduction

Chairwoman Cantwell, Vice-Chairman Barrasso, and Members of the Committee, my name is Kevin Washburn and I am the Assistant Secretary—Indian Affairs at the Department of the Interior (Department). Thank you for the opportunity to provide the Administration's statement on *Carcieri v. Salazar*[1] and the need to bring certainty to trust land acquisitions.

Restoring tribal homelands is one of this Administration's highest priorities. This Administration has repeatedly stressed the importance of and need for a *Carcieri* fix. For the past three years, the President has proposed a sensible fix to treat all tribes equally in exercising the fundamental responsibility of placing land into trust for tribes. Included as part of the budget request, the Administration's practical solution would amend the Indian Reorganization Act essentially as follows:

> Effective beginning on June 18, 1934, the term "Indian" as used in this Act shall include all persons of Indian descent who are members any federally recognized Indian tribe, and all persons who are descendants of such members who were, on June 1, 1934, residing within the present boundaries of any Indian reservation, and shall further include all other persons of one-half or more Indian blood.

Without such a fix by Congress, *Carcieri* presents a potential problem for any tribe by allowing opponents to mire routine trust applications in protracted and unnecessary litigation. As we have seen repeatedly since the decision, those challenging a trust acquisition routinely assert that a particular tribe was not under federal jurisdiction in 1934, even when such claim is clearly unsupported by the historical record. Tribes like the Oneida Tribe of Wisconsin and the St. Regis Mohawk Tribe, which entered into treaties with the United States in the 1790s, are forced to expend scarce resources defending against such claims—resources that in these difficult budgetary times could be better spent on housing, education, and public safety. The Department is also forced to expend resources both before and during litigation to defend against such spurious claims—resources that are needed for social services, protection of natural resources and implementation of treaty rights. A straightforward *Carcieri* fix would be a tremendous economic boost to Indian country, at no cost to the Federal Government.

II. *Carcieri* Conflicts with the Purposes of the Indian Reorganization Act

In *Carcieri*, the Supreme Court held that land could not be taken into trust for the Narragansett Tribe of Rhode Island under Section 5 of the Indian Reorganization Act of 1934 because the Tribe was not under Federal jurisdiction in 1934. As a result, the land could not be acquired in trust for the tribe and the tribe could not complete its low-income housing project. *Carcieri* is wholly inconsistent with the longstanding policies of the United States under the Indian Reorganization Act of 1934 of assisting tribes in establishing and protecting a land base sufficient to allow them to provide for the health, welfare, and safety of tribal members, and of treating all tribes equally for purposes of setting aside lands for tribal communities.

Our testimony is informed by history. In 1887, Congress passed the General Allotment Act with the intent of breaking up tribal reservations by dividing tribal land into 80- and 160-acre parcels for individual tribal members. The General Allotment Act resulted in huge losses of tribally owned lands, it created the *Cobell* fractional ownership problem, and it is responsible for the current "checkerboard" pattern of ownership on many Indian reservations. Approximately two-thirds of tribal lands were lost as a result of this now repudiated federal policy.

Congress enacted the Indian Reorganization Act in 1934 in part to remedy the devastating effects of these prior policies. Congress's intent in enacting the Indian Reorganization Act was three-fold: to halt the federal policy of allotment and assimilation; to reverse the negative impact of allotment policies; and to secure for all Indian tribes a land base on which to engage in economic development and self-determination.

The first section of the Indian Reorganization Act expressly discontinued the allotment of Indian lands, while the next section preserved the trust status of Indian lands. In section 3, Congress authorized the Secretary to restore tribal ownership of the remaining "surplus" lands on Indian reservations. Most importantly, Congress authorized the Secretary to secure homelands for Indian tribes by acquiring land to be held in trust for Indian tribes under section 5. That section has been called

---

[1] 555 U.S. 379 (2009).

"the capstone of the land-related provisions of the [Indian Reorganization Act]." Cohen's Handbook of Federal Indian Law § 15.07[1][a] (2005). The Act also authorized the Secretary to designate new reservations. Thus, Congress recognized that one of the key factors for tribes in developing and maintaining their economic and political strength lay in the protection of each tribe's land base. The United States Supreme Court has similarly recognized that the Indian Reorganization Act's "overriding purpose" was "to establish machinery whereby Indian tribes would be able to assume a greater degree of self-government, both politically and economically." *Morton v. Mancari*, 417 U.S. 535, 542 (1974).

This Administration fully supports and continues to implement and advance the policy goals Congress established eight decades ago of protecting and restoring tribal homelands, and advancing tribal self-determination. Acquisition of land in trust for the benefit of Indian tribes is essential to tribal self-determination and protects tribal lands for future generations. For example, trust acquisitions provide tribes the ability to enhance housing opportunities for their citizens. This is particularly necessary where many reservation economies require support from the tribal government to bolster local housing markets and offset high unemployment rates. Trust acquisitions are necessary for tribes to realize the tremendous energy development capacity that exists on their lands. Trust acquisitions allow tribes to grant certain rights of way and enter into leases that are necessary for tribes to negotiate the use and sale of their natural resources. Uncertainty regarding the trust status of land may create confusion regarding law enforcement services and interfere with the security of Indian communities. Additionally, trust lands provide the greatest protections for many communities who rely on subsistence hunting and agriculture that are important elements of tribal culture and ways of life.

III. Consequences of the *Carcieri* Decision

The harms inflicted by *Carcieri* undermine the purposes envisioned by the IRA to remedy the harms perpetrated on tribal communities by policies like the General Allotment Act of 1887. Just as Congress acted in 1934 to remedy the devastating impacts of the General Allotment Act, Congress must act today to make clear that the United States' responsibility to secure homelands extends to all tribes.

Following the *Carcieri* decision, the Department must examine whether a tribe seeking to have land acquired in trust under the Indian Reorganization Act was "under federal jurisdiction" in 1934. This is a fact-specific analysis that is conducted on a tribe-by-tribe basis. The Department must conduct this analysis for every tribe, including those tribes whose jurisdictional status is unquestioned. Because of the historical and fact-intensive nature of this inquiry, it can be time-consuming and costly for tribes and for the Department.

In the wake of the *Carcieri* decision, both the Department and many tribes have been forced to spend an inordinate amount of time analyzing whether the tribes were under Federal jurisdiction in 1934 and thus entitled to have land taken into trust. We testified before this Committee, just over a year ago, on the burdens, costs and uncertainty on the fee to trust process that resulted from the *Carcieri* decision. We stated then, and it continues to remain true, that once this analysis is completed, if the Department decides to take land into trust and provides notice of its intent, the *Carcieri* decision makes it likely that we will face costly and complex litigation over whether applicant tribes were under federal jurisdiction in 1934.

The *Carcieri* decision undermines the primary goal of Congress in enacting the Indian Reorganization Act: the acquisition of land in trust for tribes to secure a land base on which to live and engage in economic development. This decision imposes additional administrative burdens on the Department's long-standing approach to trust acquisitions and the uncertainty created by Court's decision serves to destabilize tribal economies and their surrounding communities. The Court's decision in *Patchak*,[2] further undermines tribal self-determination and self-governance by providing litigants an opportunity to challenge trust acquisitions even when the land is already held in trust.

The Administration recently promulgated a rule that implements a "patch" to address *Patchak* by clarifying that the Department will immediately place land in trust once the agency makes a final decision to take the land into trust. While the *Patchak* patch will provide some relief for the problems *Patchak* created, the *Carcieri* decision, combined with the *Patchak* decision, casts a dark cloud of uncertainty on land acquisitions for tribes under the Indian Reorganization Act, and ultimately inhibits and discourages the productive use of tribal trust land itself.

---

[2] 132 S. Ct. 2199 (2012).

IV. Conclusion

In 1934, Congress acted to correct the Federal Government's allotment and assimilation policies. Congress' action then was designed to foster tribal self-determination and economic development and in the decades that followed, the Department implemented this responsibility for all tribes. Today, the Federal Government and Indian country continue to address the present day harms that emanate from the policies of more than a century ago, yet *Carcieri* injects tangible costs and delays that impede progress in Indian country. The power to acquire lands in trust is an essential tool for the United States to effectuate its longstanding policy of fostering tribal self-determination. A system where some federally recognized tribes cannot enjoy the same rights and privileges available to other federally recognized tribes is unacceptable. The President's proposed Fiscal Year 2014 Budget includes language that, if enacted, would resolve this issue. We look forward to working with the Committee and the Congress on this matter.

This concludes my statement. I would be happy to answer questions.

The CHAIRWOMAN. Thank you. Assistant Secretary, what do you think the impact has been in taking land into trust for tribes as it relates to this self-governance issue and this trajectory? Has the Department done any studies or analysis to analyze the economic development opportunities or impacts?

Mr. WASHBURN. Well, we live with it every day. Because we now have to go through, jump through a lot more hoops to take land into trust for any tribe. We first have to do a *Carcieri* analysis to see if they are one of the tribes for whom we can take land into trust. In every case, every tribe, in other words, sort of has a *Carcieri* problem, because we have to go through this lengthy analysis to determine whether it is okay to take land into trust for them under the *Carcieri* decision.

Secondly, we are up to our eyeballs in litigation on these matters. Some in Federal district courts and some in the Interior Board of Indian Appeals, but in excess of 15 cases that we are litigating. So once again, lots of man hours being used to address this issue.

We certainly know that it also puts a damper on economic development, because there is uncertainty about tribes' land into trust applications. Those who want to finance development or that sort of thing aren't willing to do so if there is a cloud on the title, in essence.

So we have seen a lot of different problems along those lines since we have had to live with the *Carcieri* decision.

The CHAIRWOMAN. So you don't know of any particular study the Department has done about the economic impacts or loss of economic development that has happened since the *Carcieri* decision?

Mr. WASHBURN. We haven't put a battery of economists on the question. No, it is much more anecdotal. We haven't researched the issue systematically.

The CHAIRWOMAN. And how would you respond to people who say that, I know we are going to hear from people about, they think that these applications are rubber-stamped to a certain degree, or always approved. What would you say?

Mr. WASHBURN. I will push back on that. Let me first say that Congress has granted the Administration the power to restore tribal homelands, and has suggested that we should be doing so. And the President has strongly committed to restoring tribal homelands. Having said that, it is not a rubber stamp. It is true that there aren't very many disapprovals, but the reason for that is, when an application becomes problematic, usually it is withdrawn. Sometimes it is withdrawn so the tribes can talk to local governments or others more, so they can work through issues.

But we don't usually get to the point of disapproval. We usually get applications withdrawn before that would ever happen. So while it is true that applications are almost entirely approved, it is that the ones that are likely to be disapproved just get withdrawn. So it is not in fact rubber-stamped.

The CHAIRWOMAN. I am going to turn to my colleagues to see if they have any questions for you. Senator Barrasso?

Senator BARRASSO. Thank you, Madam Chair.

I do, and I heard your testimony on home ownership and communities that want to expand. The way these committees work, you testify and then there is a panel after you, and sometimes it is hard to go back to you. So I try to read the testimony, and I have been doing that for Diane Dillon who is here, Supervisor, Napa County Board of Supervisors on behalf of the California State Association of Counties. Her written testimony, and she is going to testify on the next panel, contends that there are flaws in the trust land application process.

The Chairwoman made some comments there, so local governments may comment on jurisdictional and certain other regulatory impacts arising from the trust land. But the required notice to local governments doesn't actually include the application or the proposed use of land by the tribe. And you made some reference to the fact that they didn't have to state the use.

How do you think the notice and the opportunity for impact by local communities could be improved?

Mr. WASHBURN. We have just improved that to some degree with our so-called *Patchak* patch regulations. So one of the things we do in those regulations is increase the notice that we give to people who have objected in the land into trust process, so that if they do want to challenge the decision, they get clearer notice. So one of the things we have done is, if anybody had written in during the application process, they will get personal notice afterwards, after a decision has been made, if the decision ultimately is positive, so that they can file a claim, they pursue other remedies if they like.

We do reach out directly to State and local governments to determine what their views are. We specifically ask them about tax issues, jurisdiction issues and usually environmental consequences, because there is usually a NEPA process as well. So we feel like we consult fairly heavily. We do ask for very specific information and we certainly sometimes get more than just what we have asked for, and we consider that information. So that is something that we feel like we do actually fairly well. In fact, if it is a very large development, usually the tribe has to have some sort of agreement in place with county or local governments for water treatment facilities, for road access. There are usually all kinds of agreements between governments to make these things happen.

So we feel like there is a heck of a lot of cooperation that occurs.

Senator BARRASSO. The final rules that you recently issued are to address changes in the applicability of the Quiet Title Act to trust acquisitions. They are also intended to broaden and clarify the notice of decision to acquire land into trust. Do you believe these preserve affected parties' ability to seek judicial review before the land is actually taken into trust, and what do you see the impacts are on judicial review?

Mr. WASHBURN. Thank you, Vice Chairman. Before the *Patchak* decision, the United States had always taken the view that once the land was taken into trust, there could be no action. It was in trust, and the United States had sovereign immunity, so there could be no action.

So there was a 30-day period between the decision and the actual action of taking land into trust that was instituted in 1996 to give people a chance to bring an action in court if they wished to oppose the land into trust application after it had been decided.

The *Patchak* decision sort of erased the need for that. Because now, even the land is into trust, presumably in most cases or many cases, at any rate, someone can go ahead and bring an action. So the need for the 30-day period was gone. So we got rid of that 30-day period. But objectors now have quite a bit of opportunity in the courts to pursue an action. And the courts have said in *Patchak* that there is a waiver of sovereign immunity for that action to proceed. So we don't see that the new regulation is being needed. The old regulation, the 30-day period, is not needed any longer.

Senator BARRASSO. Thank you. Thank you, Madam Chairwoman.

The CHAIRWOMAN. Senator Begich?

Senator BEGICH. Thank you very much.

I have a couple of questions and then one somewhat not related but connected. As you know, we are a little different in Alaska, with ANSCA lands and so forth. But we do have, I think we have one application going through the process total. It is a unique process we have. Our tribes also don't have a lot of resources, don't have lands, they have issues with public safety, especially around public safety, which will be the second part of my questions.

But can you tell me, and I think it is just one right now, down in Haines, Alaska, Southeast Alaska, that may be applying. Do you have any information on the status of that and what is going on with their application of land in trust?

Mr. WASHBURN. The whole question of land into trust in Alaska is in litigation right now.

Senator BEGICH. We are one of those 15 cases, I think you said 15 different cases. We are one of them. So is this one on pending that outcome?

Mr. WASHBURN. It is. The Department, this is in litigation, so that is causing the Department, well, we have to deal with the litigation, but also reassessing what does this all mean with regard to land into trust in Alaska. That is an ongoing conversation that really won't be able to be resolved until the litigation is resolved.

Senator BEGICH. And we have gone through, if I am not mistaken, the D.C. Circuit, District Court, and now it is going to the next level. Is that correct?

Mr. WASHBURN. Well, that is——

Senator BEGICH. Depending.

Mr. WASHBURN. Right.

Senator BEGICH. I should never assume. I should just assume that when one side loses, they will do something.

But let me move to a couple other questions. This is somewhat unrelated, but again, I want to emphasize my point here, and I appreciate it. I know there is not an update on the Senate side on *Carcieri* in regard to legislation, but keeping Alaska status quo is what we are interested in. I noted your comments at the beginning, I don't know if you were referring to some of the stuff that I have heard regarding Alaska. But we are trying not to make this too broad. We are adding more things to it from Alaska's perspective. I am in agreement on that from Alaska's specific issues, trying to be added in there or deleted out.

So I am not sure we are aligned, but we are aligned by that statement you made earlier. I don't know if that makes sense to you.

Mr. WASHBURN. Well, I think yes.

Senator BEGICH. We may disagree on what the outcome may be through the litigation, but I am trying to avoid any Alaska exceptions in here.

So let me go to another issue, and this is, and you may be able to respond to this, it is in regard to the Indian Law and Order Commission report that just came out. It is a pretty significant report. It is a road map for making Native Americans safer. It is thick actually in Alaska because of how bad it is. We have a whole chapter, which is somewhat amazing when you think about it. For how much trouble and how much time to put one of these reports together, then to see Alaska a whole chapter in there.

I have a letter going to the Chairwoman, I think it goes out today, asking for a special hearing in regard to this report. I think this is very telling of what we should be doing. And part of putting land into trust on a national level is to get more resources to tribes to solve some of the problems. In Alaska, we have a little bit more unique situation.

But I wanted to just pick your brain while you are here. I caught you in the hall last time, I didn't have time on another issue. But I want to pick your brain on this one in regard to this report. As you know, I have a piece of legislation that is Safe Families and Villages Act, which is focused on allowing tribes in Alaska a little more jurisdiction. Because VAWA missed Alaska tribes. That is also why I want to be very careful about *Carcieri*. Because I want to make sure that we don't have something later we have to fix. And in VAWA, we missed Alaska tribes. And we have to fix that.

Can you give me any thoughts that you might have, especially on how much you have had time to look at this report? It is pretty significant. And like I said, Alaska has a whole chapter. You actually, in a report like this don't necessarily want a chapter dedicated to you, unless it is saying all these great things. And this is not necessarily what this talks about. It talks about our lack of justice, lack of public safety efforts and many other things. Do you have any comments on what we could be doing or just some thoughts? While you are here, I figured I would take advantage of the moment.

Mr. WASHBURN. Absolutely. We do look forward to a hearing on that subject. We are digesting the report, there is a lot in that report. It is quite extensive. And certainly it is extensive on Alaska.

We have heard from a lot of Alaska tribes about the inadequacy of village public safety officers. They work really hard, but we don't give them the tools that they need.

Senator BEGICH. That is right.

Mr. WASHBURN. Serious problems, obviously, with crime control in rural villages. We are looking at that. So we are grateful that you are providing it more attention. And we do think it deserves more attention.

So we are digesting it and we would be glad to talk more about it if the Chairwoman decides to hold a hearing on this subject.

Senator BEGICH. Fantastic. Madam Chair, I am going to send you a letter I have drafted today, just asking us to consider that. I think it is an important report, a lot of good work. I know from just Alaska's perspective, I think the folks came up four different times and a lot of in-depth, good report. It is not polished up, it is here it is, here is what needs to be done, or here are the problems that we see, which I think is telling for us, especially in Indian Country, not only nationwide, but for my State of Alaska.

I will look forward to having the conversation with you. I look forward to working with the Chairwoman in regard to potentially having some discussion on this on a much broader perspective.

Mr. WASHBURN. Thank you, Senator.

The CHAIRWOMAN. Yes, thank you, Senator. Thank you for your letter.

If I could, just a couple more questions. I have looked at this analysis of land into trust just for the last couple of years. These are various applications but the majority of which are, I think there are 1,466, something like that, that were approved. The majority of which are housing, agriculture, economic development, infrastructure. I guess infrastructure includes things like habitat preservation or health care centers. In fact, I was up in Senator Begich's State this summer looking at one of these issues as it related to expanding the health center in Anchorage, and making sure that they could expand to better accommodate the issues of pregnancy and housing of families in relation to that.

But the majority of these, as I said, the majority of these are, well, it looks like a big chunk, the largest chunk, 593 out of that 1,400 is related to agriculture. Is that mining too?

Mr. WASHBURN. No, I don't believe that would be mining. But yes, it is a variety of things, honestly. But a lot of tribes are highly fractionated and checkerboarded. So much of what that is is tribes trying to reduce the checkerboard within their reservation. So it is a variety of different type things. Some of them are economic development. Some of them are grazing or farming lands.

The CHAIRWOMAN. I think we hear a lot of this discussion as it relates to gaming, and yet we want to make sure that we don't hamper what is, I mean, to me, I would love to see some economic analysis of what we have done to slow down economic development in Indian Country, given that in our State, the Port of Tacoma and the Puyallup Tribe, the Puyallup Tribe ended up taking land into trust that allowed them to expand in downtown Tacoma. They basically because of that land exchange and partnership between the City of Tacoma and Puyallup and the Port, the port expansion, it enabled Tacoma to basically overtake Seattle in being the largest container port in our State.

So this little land into trust issue is, for me in a lot of ways, it is a much bigger economic tool than whether it is going to work effectively or whether it is going to be a chilling effect. So I certainly want it work effectively, because it has been a major tool for not just Indian Country to solve problems, but for Indian Country to form partnerships within communities, to solve larger problems. So it is a very, very important business tool.

But I also wanted to just follow up on Vice Chairman Barrasso's question. Do you think there is any more that can be done to provide communities a voice in this process without diminishing their tribal sovereignty?

Mr. WASHBURN. We have heard those complaints, and that is one of the reasons we increased the notice that we provided after, when we make one of these decisions. Because we wanted to make sure that there was such notice.

The law is built to account for that voice, to bring that voice in. Part 151 requires us to notify State and local governments and then look at the information they provide us. We specifically question them about tax and jurisdiction and environmental consequences, and look at the information that those governments provide. So there is a fair bit of communication that happens with State and local governments already.

So I suspect we could always do more. Communication is vitally important. But we have built-in processes for doing that, both in our regulations and in IGRA. IGRA requires that as well.

The CHAIRWOMAN. Yes, Senator Begich?

Senator BEGICH. Just one more. You just made me think about, as a former mayor, I am just trying to think of all the developments that ever came into my city. They never work in isolation. So you are always engaged, even without the regulatory process, I mean, as I was listening to this back and forth, I am thinking to myself, I can't think of one project that just kind of like planted themselves down in our community of 1,900 square miles, that is how large the city was by size, so you can get a little visual there, and just suddenly, they are in business. It doesn't work that way.

Even if the rules weren't there, the local government is going to be engaged because of road access, water, sewer, power, even phone and cable, depending on how that relationship is in the local communities. I am just trying to think, I am anxious for the next panel, because I am trying to figure out what the fear is. I can only tell you that there is no way someone could come into a community, at least, I am thinking of Anchorage, when I was mayor, dropped in a whole development and say, we are going to do this and we are not really going to talk to you. It doesn't work that way. They want the connectivity and the cooperation because at the end of the day, there is joint use of resources.

Am I missing something here?

Mr. WASHBURN. I think you are correct. There is also law enforcement and fire, all these things that have to be dealt with. I think Supervisor Dillon is very articulate and very thoughtful and I am sure she will talk about some of those things. In my experience, there is a lot of cooperation that has to happen. You might need an exit off the freeway, you might need a lane widened, you have to have a water treatment plant. All that stuff. There is just a lot of need for that cooperation at all levels of government. And it tends to happen. You can't produce a $100 million or $500 million casino without working with the local authorities.

Senator BEGICH. I will give one last example. There is a large development by one of our regional corporations, just on the edge of what we would consider the east part of Anchorage. They were near a freeway, but it was all their land and it was pretty wide open. And it was undeveloped land and they wanted to build a large mall with multiple box stores, all kinds of things. But everything from the street sign to the stop light to the overpass to the access to the employment to the buses, all that was part of the discussion.

Because at the end of the day, for example, I remember negotiating the bus route system that went through there. Why did I do that? Because one, it was going to be a very lucrative route, because of all those employees. Second, they needed it for their employees. So we had both mutual interests here.

I had wanted a stoplight in that location forever. Well, now that they were developing it, I made them pay for it. They wanted it because it made better traffic flow.

So they couldn't just plop it down. I would not consider it like a casino, obviously, but the traffic flow is like a very busy casino, there is a lot of traffic going through there, theaters, everything. But it forced us to get some of our priorities resolved that we had been waiting for for years in a partnership.

I was just thinking about that, Madam Chair. I was interested in your conversation back and forth, and it triggered my time as mayor and how these development work.

The CHAIRWOMAN. Thank you. I thank you for helping to eliminate this issue. And again, Assistant Secretary, thank you for being here. We appreciate it and we look forward to working with you on this issue.

Mr. WASHBURN. Thank you, Madam Chairwoman.

The CHAIRWOMAN. We will call up our next panel: Ms. Jacqueline Johnson-Pata, who is Executive Director of the National Congress of American Indians; the Honorable Marshall Pierite, Chairman of the Tunica-Biloxi Tribe of Louisiana; and Ms. Diane Dillon, Supervisor, Napa County Board of Supervisors, on behalf of the California State Association of Counties.

Welcome to all of you. Thank you for being here. We appreciate it. And Ms. Johnson-Pata, we will start with you.

STATEMENT OF JACQUELINE JOHNSON–PATA, EXECUTIVE DIRECTOR, NATIONAL CONGRESS OF AMERICAN INDIANS

Ms. JOHNSON-PATA. [Greeting in Native tongue.] On behalf of the National Congress of American Indians, I would like to thank you for first of all, having this hearing, which is so important to Indian Country, regarding the Supreme Court decision of *Carcieri v. Salazar*.

Before I get started, I would like to recognize Randy Notka and Hiawatha, who are here from the Narragansett Tribe. As you know, this issue stemmed from them wanting to take land into trust for housing. And here we are today, so many years later, still dealing with an issue that is just core to Indian Country.

NCAI has been asking Congress to amend the Indian Reorganization Act since the Supreme Court decision in 2009. And our concerns about the decision are coming to pass. At least 18 pending cases where tribes and the Secretary of Interior are under challenge. And then there are many more tribes whose land into trust applications, whether they are for housing, economic development, health care centers, have just been stalled while the Department works through the legal and historical analysis which is now required.

There is also concern that the litigation will grow. The IRA is a comprehensive piece of legislation that provides for tribal constitutions and tribal business structures and serves as the framework for tribal self-government. Future litigation could threaten tribal organizations, contracts, loans, tribal reservation and land, and also the provision of services. Litigation also may come from criminal defendants seeking to avoid Federal or tribal jurisdiction that would negatively impact our public safety.

We feel that this will continue to get worse until Congress acts to clarify that all federally recognized tribes are eligible under the IRA. At the same time, I want to make it clear to the county government representatives that this s not an opportunity for changes to Federal law that will place decision-making authority into county hands. The Federal Government and the Secretary of Interior have a trust responsibility to provide for the future of Indian tribes. While local government issues are considered by the Secretary under the regulatory process, and we heard that from Kevin Washburn today, at 25 C.F.R. 151, tribal leaders will never accept a legislative proposal that will transfer authority to State or county governments.

This issue starts with the history where States and counties took huge parcels of land from Indian tribes. And we need the Federal Government to protect the rights of tribes to recover land for their own tribal self-determination.

We have a vision for Indian Country and Indian people. Indian lands should be places where the old ways are maintained, where our languages are spoken, where our children learn their traditions and pass them on to the next generation. And at the same time, our vision includes a modern vision of modern life, economic development to sustain our people, safety and respectful relationships with our neighbors and the blessings of education, health care and modern technology to help us thrive.

This vision was shared by the U.S. Congress in 1934 when it passed one of the most important Federal laws in the history of our Country, the Indian Reorganization Act. With the IRA, Congress renewed its trust responsibility to protect and to restore tribal homelands, and the Indian way of life. Prior to 1934, the Federal policy toward Indian tribes was to sell off tribal land base and assimilate Indian people. The Federal Government did everything that it could to disband our people, our tribes, break up our families and suppress our culture. And as you stated earlier in your opening remarks, over 90 million acres of tribal land held under treaties was taken, more than two-thirds of our tribal land base. And the remaining lands often had very little value.

By the early 1930s, the Allotment and the Assimilation Act policies were widely recognized as failures. And in 1934, Congress rejected the Allotment and Assimilation and passed the IRA. It had clear and overriding purposes that Congress would reestablish and restore tribal governments.

So 75 years later, here we are. The IRA is just as necessary as it was then. I would like to raise two important points. First, while some controversies exist, the vast majority of Indian land acquisitions taken into place in extremely rural areas are not controversial in any way. And second, State and local governments have a role in land into trust process. Under the current processes, the Interior regulation provides opportunities for all parties that are concerned about it to be heard, and to place the burden on the tribes to justify the land into trust acquisition. The regulations provide a forum for State and local communities to raise these concerns. And I believe there is time in that process to engage in ample, constructive dialogue with tribes in the most sensible and mutually agreeable options for restoring land.

I would like to thank the Committee for taking a close look at this issue today and helping us move forward the *Carcieri* fix. Thank you for all your diligent efforts on this and so many issues that face you every single day, and your representation for Indian Country. [Phrase in Native tongue.]

[The prepared statement of Mr. Johnson-Pata follows:]

PREPARED STATEMENT OF JACQUELINE JOHNSON-PATA, EXECUTIVE DIRECTOR, NATIONAL CONGRESS OF AMERICAN INDIANS

On behalf of the National Congress of American Indians, thank you for the Committee's hearing regarding the adverse implications of the U.S. Supreme Court's decision in *Carcieri v. Salazar*. As you know, the *Carcieri* decision has called into question the Department of Interior's longstanding interpretation of law regarding the Indian Reorganization Act of 1934 (IRA) and sets up unfair treatment of Indian tribes. We urge Congress to reinstate the principle that all federally recognized Indian tribes are eligible for the benefits of the IRA. Our testimony will also discuss general principles relating to the Secretary's authority to acquire land in trust for Indian tribes. Under the U.S. Constitution, all Indian tribes who had maintained tribal relations were ''under federal jurisdiction'' in 1934

Legislative Action Needed to Address *Carcieri v. Salazar*

As you know, NCAI has been asking Congress to amend the IRA since the Supreme Court decision in 2009. Our concerns about the decision are coming to pass. There are at least eighteen pending cases where tribes and the Secretary of Interior are under challenge. There are more tribes whose land to trust applications have been stalled while the Department of Interior works through painstaking legal and historical analysis. We are seeing harassment litigation against tribes who were on treaty reservations in 1934. Land acquisitions are delayed. Lending and credit are threatened. Jobs are lost or never created.

We are also concerned that the litigation will grow. The IRA is comprehensive legislation that provides for tribal constitutions and tribal business structures, and serves as a framework for tribal self-government. Future litigation could threaten tribal organizations, contracts and loans, tribal reservations and lands, and provision of services. Ancillary attacks may also come from criminal defendants seeking to avoid federal or tribal jurisdiction, and would negatively affect public safety on reservations. We fear that this could continue to get worse until Congress acts to clarify that all federally recognized tribes are eligible for the IRA.

At the same time I want to make it clear to county government representatives that this is not an opportunity for changes to federal law that will place decision-making authority in county hands. The Federal Government and the Secretary of the Interior have the trust responsibility to provide for the future of Indian tribes. While local government issues are considered by the Secretary under the regulatory process at 25 CFR 151, tribal leaders will never accept a legislative proposal that transfers authority to state or county governments. This issue starts with a history where states and counties took huge amounts of land from Indian tribes, and we need the federal government to protect our right to recover land for tribal self-determination.

We have a vision for our future as Indian people. Indian lands should be places where the old ways are maintained, our languages are spoken, and our children learn our traditions and pass them on to the next generation. At the same time, this vision includes modern life—economic development to sustain our people; safety and respectful relationships with our neighbors; and the blessings of education, healthcare and modern technology to help us thrive.

This vision was shared by the U.S. Congress in 1934 when it passed one of the most important federal laws in the history of our country—the Indian Reorganization Act. With the IRA, Congress renewed its trust responsibility to protect and restore our tribal homelands and the Indian way of life. Four and a half years ago, the shared vision and the federal responsibility to Indian tribes were threatened by the Supreme Court's interpretation of the IRA in *Carcieri v. Salazar*.

Prior to 1934, the Federal Government policy toward Indian tribes was to sell off the tribal land base and assimilate Indian people. The federal government did everything it could to disband our tribes, break up our families, and suppress our culture. Over 90 million acres of tribal land held under treaties were taken, more than two thirds of the tribal land base, and the remaining lands were often of little value. By the early 1930's the allotment and assimilation policies were widely recognized as failures. The policies did little more than inflict great suffering on Indian people and dishonor our Nation.

In 1934, Congress rejected allotment and assimilation and passed the IRA. The clear and overriding purpose of Congress was to re-establish the tribal land base and restore tribal governments that had withered under prior federal policies. The legislative history and the Act itself are filled with references to restoration of federal support for tribes that had been cut off, and "to provide land for landless Indians."

A problem with our legal system is that lawyers sometimes lose sight of the fundamental history and purpose of a law, debate the meaning of a few words, and suddenly the law is turned on its head. Today, because of the *Carcieri* decision, we have opponents arguing that tribes are not eligible for the benefits of the IRA if they were not under active federal supervision by the Bureau of Indian Affairs in 1934, or if they did not have lands in trust 1934. Both of these arguments are contrary to the history and purpose of the law to re-establish federal support for tribes that had been abandoned or ignored by the BIA, and to restore land to tribes that had little or no land.

Today, 75 years later—the IRA is just as necessary as it was in 1934. The purposes of the IRA were frustrated, first by WWII and then by the Termination Era. The work did not begin again until the 1970's with the Self-Determination Policy, and since then Indian tribes are building economies from the ground up, and must earn every penny to buy back their own land. Still today, many tribes have no land base and many tribes have insufficient lands to support housing and self-government and culture. We will need the IRA for many more years until the tribal needs for self-support and self-determination are met.

U.S. Constitution Creates Presumption of Federal Jurisdiction over Indian Tribes

Carcieri v. Salazar involved a challenge by the State of Rhode Island to the authority of the Secretary to take land in to trust for the Narragansett Tribe under Section 465 of the Indian Reorganization Act (IRA). The opinion involves the definition of "Indian" in Section 479:

25 U.S.C. § 479

The term "Indian" as used in this Act shall include all persons of Indian descent who are members of any recognized Indian tribe *now under Federal jurisdiction*, and all persons who are descendants of such members who were, on June 1, 1934, residing within the present boundaries of any Indian reservation, and shall further include all other persons of one-half or more Indian blood. For the purposes of this Act Eskimos and other aboriginal peoples of Alaska shall be considered Indians. The term "tribe" wherever used in this Act shall be construed to refer to any Indian tribe, organized band, pueblo, or the Indians residing on one reservation. The words "adult Indians" wherever used in this Act shall be construed to refer to Indians who have attained the age of twenty-one years. (emphasis added.)

The Supreme Court's decision reversed the 1st Circuit and held that the term "now" limits the authority of the Secretary to only take land in trust for Indian tribes that were under federal jurisdiction on June 18, 1934, the date the IRA was enacted. The Court accepted the State of Rhode Island's assertion that the Narragansett Tribe was not "under federal jurisdiction" in 1934.

After the *Carcieri* decision, the phrase "under federal jurisdiction" takes on greater legal significance in the land to trust process and in all applications of the IRA. The Secretary of Interior is faced with questions of whether an Indian tribe was "under federal jurisdiction" on a date nearly eighty years ago—a period of time when federal administration was highly decentralized and for which record keeping was often inconsistent. After significant research into the legislative history of the IRA, NCAI strongly urges both Congress and the Administration to recognize the constitutional roots of federal jurisdiction in Indian affairs. The Department of Interior can and should narrowly interpret the *Carcieri* decision, and NCAI strongly urges Congress to reaffirm the principle of equal treatment of all federally recognized tribes—because it is rooted in our federal Constitution.

Although the nature of federal Indian law has varied significantly during the course of U.S. history, there is a central principle that has remained constant: jurisdiction over Indian affairs is delegated to the federal government in the U.S. Constitution. The authority is derived from the Indian Commerce Clause, the Treaty Clause, the Territory and Property Clause, and the trust relationship created in treaties, course of dealings and the Constitution's adoption of inherent powers necessary to regulate military and foreign affairs. *See, United States v. Lara*, 541 U.S. 193 (2004).

Federal jurisdiction over Indian tribes is limited by legal principles that were at the forefront of Congressional consideration in 1934, although they are not in frequent use today. During Allotment Era prior to 1934, Congress passed laws that created U.S. citizenship and allotments of private property for tribal Indians. Questions arose on whether those citizens could be treated legally as "Indians" for the purposes of the federal Indian laws. There was a significant string of Supreme Court cases that dealt with these questions, primarily in the context of the federal criminal laws and liquor control laws related to Indians, and restrictions on alienation and taxation of Indian property. *See, Hallowell v. United States*, 221 U.S. 317 (1911); *Tiger v. Western Invest. Co.*, 221 U.S. 286 (1911); *United States v. Rickert*, 188 U.S. 432 (1903); *United States v. Celestine*, 215 U.S. 278 (1909); *United States v. Sandoval*; 231 U.S. 28 (1913); *Matter of Heff*, 197 U.S. 488 (1905) overruled by *United States v. Nice*, 241 U.S. 591 (1916); *U.S. v. Ramsey*, 271 U.S. 467 (1926).

The holding of these decisions is that Indian tribes and Indian people remain under federal jurisdiction unless they have ceased tribal relations or federal supervision has been terminated by treaty or act of Congress. *See, U.S. v. Nice*, 241 U.S. 591, 598 (1916), "the tribal relation may be dissolved and the national guardianship brought to an end; but it rests with Congress to determine when and how this shall be done, and whether the emancipation shall at first be complete or only partial." "The Constitution invested Congress with power to regulate traffic in intoxicating liquors with the Indian tribes, meaning with the individuals composing them. That was a continuing power of which Congress could not devest itself. It could be exerted at any time and in various forms during the continuance of the tribal relation . . . ." Id at 600.

The origins of this constitutional legal doctrine are summarized in Cohen's Handbook of Federal Indian Law (2005 ed.) § 14.01[2–3], regarding the prior status of non-citizen Indians and efforts to assimilate Indians and terminate their tribal status. In this era the Supreme Court repeatedly affirmed Congress's authority to terminate federal guardianship, but found that Congress retained jurisdiction over Indians despite allotment of tribal lands and the grant of U.S. citizenship to Indians so long as tribal relations were maintained.

The exclusion of Indians who had ceased tribal relations was a significant limitation on the scope of the IRA. During the Allotment Era, Indian tribes were under severe pressures from federal policies and warfare, extermination efforts, disease and dislocation. Some tribes had become fragmented and were no longer maintaining a social or political organization.

This understanding comports with the unique legislative history of the phrase "now under federal jurisdiction" in Section 479. During a legislative hearing in 1934 when Commissioner of Indian Affairs John Collier was presenting the IRA to the Senate Committee on Indian Affairs, he was asked by Senator Burton Wheeler, the Chairman of the Committee, whether the legislation would apply to Indian people who were no longer in a tribal organization. Collier responded by suggesting the insertion of the terms "now under Federal jurisdiction." See, Senate Committee on Indian Affairs, *To Grant Indians the Freedom to Organize*, 73rd Cong., 2nd Session, 1934, 265–266. By inserting these terms, Congress excluded the members of tribes who had ceased tribal relations. As discussed in the hearing record, those tribal members could only gain the benefits of the IRA if they met the definition under the "half-blood" provisions. Commissioner Collier submitted a brief to the Committee that reiterated the principles of broad federal jurisdiction in Indian affairs under the Constitution. Id at 265. This brief specifically quoted the Supreme Court's decision in *United States v. Sandoval*, 231 U.S. 28 at 46 (1913):

> *Not only does the Constitution expressly authorize Congress to regulate commerce with the Indian tribes, but long continued legislative and executive usage and an unbroken current of judicial decisions have attributed to the United States as a superior and civilized nation the power and the duty of exercising a fostering care and protection over all dependent Indian communities within its borders, whether within its original territory or territory subsequently acquired, and whether within or without the limits of a state.*

The practices and regulations of the Bureau of Indian Affairs regarding the establishment of recognition for American Indian tribes, found in 25 C.F.R. Pt. 83, are also based on these legal principles. 25 C.F.R. Pt. 83.7(b) and (c) are the requirements of continued tribal relations. 25 C.F.R. 83.7(g) is the requirement that tribal status and federal relations have not been revoked by Congress. Any tribe recognized pursuant to Part 83 has already received a factual determination that the tribe was under federal jurisdiction in 1934. The only other available methods for organizing under the IRA are to be recognized as Indians of one-half or more Indian blood, or to receive federal recognition directly from Congress.

In short, the *Carcieri* decision's requirement that an Indian tribe must be "under federal jurisdiction" in 1934 should not place a burden of proof on the tribe to demonstrate that federal jurisdiction existed or was actively exercised at that time. The presumption under the Constitution is that federal jurisdiction over tribes always exists unless it has been completely and equivocally revoked by an Act of Congress, or tribal relations have ceased. Because the practices and regulations of the BIA regarding federal recognition already include these exclusions, and have prevented the recognition of tribes that have failed to maintain tribal relations, there are no federally recognized tribes which were not "under federal jurisdiction" in 1934.

The Secretary of the Interior's Authority and Responsibility to Restore Land in Trust for Indian Tribes

The principal goal of the Indian Reorganization Act was to halt and reverse the abrupt decline in the economic, cultural, governmental and social well-being of Indian tribes caused by the disastrous federal policy of "allotment" and sale of reservation lands. Between the years of 1887 and 1934, the U.S. Government took more than 90 million acres from the tribes without compensation, nearly 2/3 of all reservation lands, and sold it to settlers and timber and mining interests. The IRA is comprehensive legislation for the benefit of tribes that stops the allotment of tribal lands, provides for the acquisition of new lands, continues the federal trust ownership of tribal lands, encourages economic development, and provides a framework for the reestablishment of tribal government institutions on their own lands.

In contemporary implementation of trust land acquisition, we would like to raise three important points. *First*, while some controversies exist, what is often misunderstood is that the vast majority of trust land acquisitions take place in extremely rural areas and are not controversial in any way. Most acquisitions involve home sites of 30 acres or less within reservation boundaries. Trust land acquisition is also necessary for consolidation of fractionated and allotted Indian lands, which most often are grazing, forestry or agricultural lands. Other typical acquisitions include land for Indian housing, health care clinics that serve both Indian and non-Indian communities, and land for Indian schools.

Second, state and local governments have a role in the land to trust process. The Interior regulations provide opportunities for all concerned parties to be heard, and place the burden on tribes to justify the trust land acquisition, particularly in the off-reservation context. It is important to recognize that land issues require case by case balancing of the benefits and costs unique to a particular location and community. The regulations cannot be expected to anticipate every situation that might arise, but they do provide an ample forum for local communities to raise opposition to a particular acquisition and they reinforce the Secretary's statutory authority to reject any acquisition. State and local governments have an opportunity to engage in constructive dialogue with tribes on the most sensible and mutually agreeable options for restoring Indian land. In most cases, there is strong community support for the development of tribal schools, housing, health care clinics, and economic development ventures that will benefit surrounding communities as well as the tribe.

Third, the chief problem with the land to trust process is the interminable delays caused by inaction at the Bureau of Indian Affairs. Too often have tribes spent scarce resources to purchase land and prepare a trust application only to have it sit for years or even decades without a response. In addition, during inordinate delays tribes risk losing funding and support for the projects that they have planned for the land, and environmental review documents grow stale. Tribal leaders have encouraged the BIA to establish internal time lines and checklists so that tribes will have a clear idea of when a decision on their application will be rendered. Tribes should know if progress is being made at all, and, if not, why not. While there have been some recent improvements in the process, the issue evokes great frustration over pending applications and has been raised by tribal leaders at every NCAI meeting.

Conclusion

While it is important for the Interior Department to properly apply the principles we have discussed here, many tribes (and the federal government) would still be subject to litigation that could create uncertainty and delay tribal progress for years to come. Legislation to address *Carcieri* is the only way to provide the certainty needed to avoid that wasteful result. NCAI urges the Committee to work closely with Indian tribes and the Administration on legislation to address *Carcieri* and allow all federally recognized Indian tribes to enjoy the benefits of the IRA. We thank you for your diligent efforts on behalf of Indian country on these and many other issues.

The CHAIRWOMAN. Thank you, and thank you for your testimony.

We will next turn to the Honorable Marshall Pierite. Thank you so much for being here.

STATEMENT OF HON. MARSHALL PIERITE, CHAIRMAN, TUNICA–BILOXI TRIBE OF LOUISIANA; CHAIR, USET CARCIERI TASK FORCE

Mr. PIERITE. Thank you. First I want to give all honor, all praise and all the glory to God the Father, the Son and Holy Spirit.

Good afternoon, Madam Chairman, Senator Begich. I am Chairman of the Tunica-Biloxi Tribe and serve as chair of the USET *Carcieri* Task Force. Thank you for this opportunity to testify today.

First and foremost, I want to touch on your opening comments, Madam Chairwoman, when you said we need to shed light on this issue. We need to shed a light on all issues and concerns, because when we shed a light, faith is born. And faith is born always during the light.

It also is developed in the darkness. And Native American culture is strong in faith, because we dwelled in the darkness for centuries. I just wanted to make that comment.

Despite the many contributions and personal sacrifices that Native Americans have made to the Nation, the United States has a miserable record of keeping faith with tribal governments. The history of theft, neglect and broken laws and treaties has led to hard feelings for Native Americans and non-Natives alike.

Today, however, I would like to highlight what happens when tribal governments utilize their unique legal position to benefit themselves and how this is also good for their non-Indian neighbors. Unfortunately, the U.S. Supreme Court *Carcieri* decision has cast doubt on the sovereign control of tribal lands and slowed the Federal Government's ability to place land into trust for the benefit of tribal government. Until Congress amends the Indian Reorganization Act to correct the problems created by the *Carcieri* decision, the benefits brought on by strong tribal governments for themselves and their surrounding local community will be significantly diminished.

While I do not want to dwell on the sad history of injustice against tribes and Native Americans, it is important to remember this history in order to illuminate the justice and healing that tribal reacquisition can bring. All tribes held title to large amounts of amount that has been stolen from them. Ours is merely one example.

At the time of the Louisiana Purchase treaty in 1803, the Tunica-Biloxi tribe held title to well over 50 square miles of land. But in 1980, however, the tribe controlled less than 200 acres. These lands were stolen in hundreds of small ways. But one example stands out. In 1841, Chief Melancon confronted a local landowner whose work crew was moving his fence posts into Tunica land. As the Chief protested and began removing the fence posts, the landowner shot Chief Melancon in the head in full sight of many witnesses. The common view at the time was that Indians were savages who could not farm their land properly and therefore had no right to keep it. As a result, the killer was thought to be within his rights and never stood trial.

Against this history of injustice, the Tunica-Biloxi Tribe and hundreds of other tribes across the country are utilizing their own resources to purchase land that has been stolen from them. But we do not wish to continue the cycle of mistrust, envy and hard feelings. Instead, we have forged new positive relationships with the local non-Indian communities that have grown up around us.

Utilizing our status as a sovereign nation, the Tunica-Biloxi Tribe has created several economic development enterprises that generate revenue for the tribal government to protect and enhance the welfare and culture of our tribal citizens. But they also provide major benefits for our non-Indian neighbors and revenues for State and local governments in the region.

For example, our tribal enterprises purchases over $10 million per year from local and non-Indian vendors and supplies wages in excess of $26 million per year to mostly non-Indian employees, resulting in State and Federal employment taxes of over $2 million per year. In addition, we have donated over $3 million to local charities and controlled over $25 million to the local parish government to help cover the cost associated with the additional demands facing the community from the increased economic activity.

When the tribe casino gaming as a means for economic advancement in the early 1990s, unemployment rates in Avoyelles Parish was as high as 17 percent, almost twice the national average. Local governments struggled to provide even the most basic services and it looked as if there was nothing on the horizon that might change the dismal forecast for the area.

Today, I am very proud to say that Tunica-Biloxi employs nearly 1,700 people, the vast majority of them are non-Indians. After our gaming facility opened in 1994, the direct and indirect jobs created by the Tribe caused the unemployment rate in Avoyelles Parish to drop below the national average. Home prices increased. New roads were paved. Schools improved. Parish government service expanded and hundreds of new businesses sprang up in nearby Louisiana.

Of course, many of our tribal citizens who suffered from the bitter yoke of poverty were helped as well, a first step as one of renewal for the entire region, all of our citizens and neighbors. Tribal governments across the Country are working hard to diversify our economies away from gaming and find new ways to provide the revenues we need to support our community. We hope and pray to create new manufacturing facilities, enter the software and service industry and build new clean energy projects. In order to do this, we must first repurchase the land that was stolen from us and place that land back into trust.

In light of the often-brutal history of relationships between tribes and their neighbors, the level of acrimony we often hear from non-Indians who are opposed to tribal economic development projects is not entirely surprising. I am hopeful, however, that the lessons we are learning today will yield a new spirit of cooperation and unity and that non-Indians who are fearful of tribal economic development will come to realize that what is good for our tribal nations is good for them as well.

The Supreme Court decision in *Carcieri v. Salazar* was a major step backward in the process of justice and healing. The ruling has slowed economic growth and job creation and continues to spawn legal impediments to the repatriation of Indian homelands. For the good of the tribes and generations yet to come, and for the good of our non-Indian neighbors and the Nation as a whole, Congress should act swiftly to amend the Indian Reorganization Act to conform to its original intended purposes for Native American Country and non-Native American alike, to walk in the same light. Amen.

Thank you.

[The prepared statement of Mr. Pierite follows:]

PREPARED STATEMENT OF HON. MARSHALL PIERITE, CHAIRMAN, TUNICA-BILOXI TRIBE OF LOUISIANA; CHAIR, USET CARCIERI TASK FORCE

Chairwoman Cantwell, Vice Chairman Barrasso, and members of the Committee, my name is Marshall Pierite. I am the Chairman of the Tunica-Biloxi Tribe of Louisiana and serve as Chair of the USET *Carcieri* Task Force. Thank you for this opportunity to testify before you today.

The United South and Eastern Tribes, Inc. (USET), is an inter-tribal organization representing 26 federally recognized Tribes from Texas across to Florida and up to Maine. The USET Tribes are within the Eastern Region and Southern Plains Region of the Bureau of Indian Affairs (BIA) and the Nashville Area Office of Indian Health Services (IHS), covering a large expanse of land and area compared to the Tribes in other Regions. USET Tribes can be found from the Canadian Border in Maine and New York, along the east coast to Florida, west into Mississippi and south into Texas.

Due to this large geographic area, the Tribal Nations in our region have incredible diversity. From an economic standpoint, some of our member tribes have highly developed economies, while others remain mired in poverty. All of our tribes, however, look to the United States to live up to its trust responsibility and to promote and protect our inherent Tribal sovereignty. I am here before you today, to state unequivocally, that the *Carcieri* decision is a direct infringement to the sovereignty rights for all Tribal Nations across the United States. This decision has resulted in the inability of our trustee to fulfill its trust obligations, has created two classes of sovereignty, and has presented a major barrier and challenge in our ability to pursue economic growth and prosperity.

Over the years, many witnesses have come before this committee to assert the rights of tribes and to detail the legal obligations of the federal government to protect and promote effective tribal governments. Unfortunately, the history of the

United States in meeting these obligations is full of broken treaties and statutes. Despite the myriad major contributions and personal sacrifices that tribes and Native Americans have made to the nation, the United States has a miserable record of keeping even the most basic of its promises to tribal governments.

This history of neglect and disdain has led to hard feelings for both Native Americans and non-natives alike. In some cases a level of mistrust has developed that is deeply ingrained on both sides. Today however, instead of focusing on this troubling past, I would like to highlight the success of my tribe as an example of what happens when tribal governments utilize their unique legal position to benefit not only the welfare of tribal citizens, but also the welfare of their non-Indian neighbors. The lesson of the last several decades that hundreds of tribes and local communities are learning is that strong tribal governments and the economic activity that they develop is good for both tribal communities and their non-Indian neighbors. Provided the right legal landscape, tribal governments are strong engines of economic and civic growth, and are good partners to non-Indian local communities.

Unfortunately, the U.S. Supreme Court's 2009 decision in *Carcieri v. Salazar* has cast doubt on the sovereign control of Indian lands and slowed the federal government's ability to place land into trust for the benefit of tribal governments. This complication not only harms the ability of tribes to provide for the welfare of their citizens-it also hampers the ability of tribes to bring the benefits of their economic development activities to their non-Indian neighbors. Until Congress corrects the Indian Reorganization Act in such a way as to correct the problems created by the *Carcieri* decision, the successes and benefits brought on by strong tribal governments will be significantly diminished.

While I do not want to dwell on the sad history of injustice against tribes and Native Americans, it is important to note some important parts of this history as it relates to land ownership, in order to illuminate the justice and healing that tribal land reacquisition can engender. Every tribe has its own history of loss, and every federally-recognized tribe once held title to large amounts of land that has been stolen from them. There are numerous stories across the country about the theft of Indian land and resources, and even of the killing of our people. Ours is merely one example.

Prior to the acquisition of our land by the United States through the Louisiana Purchase Treaty in 1803, the Tunica-Biloxi Tribe had been granted a "league squared" around each one of its villages by the King of Spain. Accordingly, the tribe held title to well over 50 square miles of land at that time. Like all other Spanish land grants, this land ownership was recognized by the United States in the Louisiana Purchase Treaty, and per the Trade and Intercourse Acts, these Indian lands could not be legally removed from tribal ownership without approval of the Federal Government. However, despite no approval for land transfer by the U.S. Congress in the intervening years, by 1980 the tribe controlled less than 200 acres of land.

These lands were stolen in hundreds of small ways, but one example stands out. In 1841, Chief Melacon confronted a local land owner whose work crew was moving his fence posts onto Tunica land. As the Chief began removing the fence posts the land owner shot Chief Melacon in the head in view of several other tribal citizens and non-Indians. The killer never stood trial, as the common view at the time among non-Indians in the area was that the Indians were savages who did not farm their land "properly" and therefore had no right to keep it.

Against this history of injustice, the Tunica-Biloxi Tribe, and hundreds of other tribes across the country, are utilizing their own resources to purchase land that has been stolen from them. But, we do not wish to continue the cycle of mistrust, envy and hard feelings. Instead, we have forged new positive relationships with the local non-Indian communities that have grown up around us. Utilizing our status as a sovereign nation, the Tunica-Biloxi Tribe has created several economic development enterprises. These businesses generate revenue for the tribal government to protect and enhance the welfare and culture of the tribal citizens. However, they also provide major benefits for our non-Indian neighbors and revenues for state and local governments in the region. For example, our tribal enterprises purchase over $10 million per year from local non-Indian vendors, and supply wages in excess of $26 million dollars per year to mostly non-Indian employees, resulting in state and federal employment taxes of over $2 million per year. In addition, we have donated millions of dollars to local charities, and have paid the local Parish government over $25 million to help cover the costs associated with the additional demands placed on the community from the increased economic activity.

The Tunica-Biloxi Tribe is located near the small town of Marksville in Central Louisiana. Despite a population of less than 6,000, Marksville serves as the seat of the Avoyelles parish government. When the Tribe began looking at gaming as a means for economic advancement in the early 1990s unemployment rates in

Avoyelles Parish were as high as 15–17 percent (compared to the national rate at the time of about 8 percent). Youth were leaving the area as fast as they could, and those unable to leave had no employment options. Local governments struggled to provide even the most basic services, and it looked as if there was nothing on the horizon that might change the dismal forecast for the area.

While the population of Marksville has not changed much in 20 years, the Tunica-Biloxi Tribe, through its several economic development enterprises, employs nearly 1,500 people—the vast majority of them non-Indian. After our gaming facility opened in 1995, the direct and indirect jobs created by the Tribe caused the unemployment rate in Avoyelles Parish to drop to about 6 percent. Home prices increased, new roads were paved, schools improved, Parish government services expanded, and hundreds of new businesses sprung up in Marksville and across the parish. Of course, our tribal citizens who had previously suffered greatly from economic hardship were helped as well, but the full story is one of renewal for the entire region and all of our citizens and neighbors.

Today, the Tunica-Biloxi Tribe, and hundreds of other tribal governments across the country are working hard to diversify our economies and find new enterprises that can provide the revenues we need to support our communities and protect and enhance our unique cultures. Tribes, including ours, are hoping to create new manufacturing facilities, enter the software and services industries, and build new clean energy projects. Because of the loss of our land base, in order to create these new economic development projects we must first repurchase the land that was stolen from us.

Further, in order to take advantage of the benefits of our sovereignty, we must have that land added back into the trust status from which it was originally removed. Often, purchasing the tribe's original land is not an option. In some cases this is because the tribe was removed and sent a long way from their traditional homelands. In other cases the current owners are simply not willing to sell, or the land is no longer suitable for the intended purpose due to other development, environmental degradation, or any number of other reasons. Regardless of the location of the repurchased land, the inability of tribes to swiftly have these lands placed into trust by the U.S. Department of the Interior has dramatically decreased the ability of tribal governments to create new economic opportunities and jobs for our own tribal citizens and our neighbors. We realize that we cannot fully recreate what was lost. We can strive, however, to create a better world and better lives for our children.

In light of the complicated and often brutal history of relationships between tribes and their neighbors, the level of acrimony we often hear from non-Indians who are opposed to tribal economic development projects is not entirely surprising. What I hope all of us will come to recognize, however, is that tribes and their neighbors are in this together. We must realize that we rely on each other, and all parties want the larger community and the nation to prosper. I am hopeful that the lessons we are learning in Central Louisiana and in hundreds of other communities across the country will yield a new spirit of cooperation, and that non-Indians who are fearful of tribal economic development will come to realize that what is good for our tribal communities is good for them as well.

The Supreme Court decision in *Carcieri v. Salazar* was a major step backward in this process of justice and healing. The ruling confused both tribal governments and non-Indians alike, slowed economic growth and job creation, and continues to spawn legal impediments to the repatriation of Indian homelands. For the good of tribes, for the good of Indian children and generations yet to come, and for the good of our non-Indian neighbors and the nation as a whole, Congress should act to amend the Indian Reorganization Act to conform to its original intended purpose.

The CHAIRWOMAN. Thank you, Mr. Chairman. Thank you for being here. Thank you for representing the Tunica-Biloxi Tribe so well. We appreciate it.

Ms. Dillon, thank you for being here. We are looking forward to your testimony. You can begin.

STATEMENT OF DIANE DILLON, SUPERVISOR, NAPA COUNTY BOARD OF SUPERVISORS; MEMBER, CALIFORNIA STATE ASSOCIATION OF COUNTIES

Ms. DILLON. Thank you very much.

Chairwoman, Senator Begich, thank you for the opportunity to address you today. My name is Diane Dillon and I serve on the Napa County Board of Supervisors. The testimony I am delivering today is on behalf of the California State Association of Counties, known as CSAC, of which I am an active member. Fifty-eight counties, almost 300 elected officials, representing the entire population of California, one-tenth of the U.S. population. Everyone who lives in a city lives in a county as well.

I am also submitting for the record a statement from the National Association of Counties, NACO. CSAC works closely with NACO on a number of issues, including several key Indian affairs matters.

In the brief time that I have before you today, I will describe what CSAC believes are major deficiencies in the Department of Interior's fee to trust process and provide the Committee with our recommendations for addressing these flaws. County governments have long been frustrated with the process by which lands are taken into trust. We believe the fee to trust system is broken and broken for al parties. A so-called simple *Carcieri* fix, as advocated by some stakeholders, would do nothing to repair the underlying problems in the trust land process and would serve only to perpetuate the conflict inherent in the current system.

As county governments, the people we serve are heavily impacted by fee to trust decisions. In California alone, there are currently 113 federally recognized tribes. As Senator Feinstein mentioned, there are 70 casinos. Apart from the removal of trust lands from the local tax base and land use jurisdiction, which as Secretary Washburn described, are the two issues upon which we are consulted, trust acquisitions increase demands for law enforcement, fire protection, health and social services, transportation, water and other resources provided by counties without providing any mitigation for the burdens created.

These challenges are of particular concern because newly sought-after tribal lands are targeted in well-established communities that are closer to large urban populations than existing casinos. These newly sought tribal land applications are aimed at creating new gamblers, as well as drawing business from existing casinos.

Although trust acquisitions can result in these significant off-reservation impacts, the Department of Interior does not provide impacted local governments and communities with sufficient notice regarding fee to trust applications. Further, the Department does not accord county concerns adequate weight in the land into trust process.

Many of these deficiencies in the trust land process were recently documented in a Pepperdine law review quantitative analysis of all 111 fee to trust decisions by the Pacific Region Bureau of Indian Affairs office between 2001 and 2011. The analysis found that the BIA granted 100 percent of the acquisition requests, and in no case did any Section 151 weigh against approval of an application.

Because of the lack of clear guidance and objective criteria for analyzing trust land requests, the Pacific Region BIA decisions did not give due consideration to the issues at stake.

Perhaps most egregious is that as determinations are made regarding whether property qualifies as Indian lands under the Indian Gaming Regulatory Act, which is critical to a gaming application, counties are not notified of such determination, not consulted and not invited to participate in the process. We believe that local government participation is essential in order to ensure there is a complete factual basis upon which objective decisions can be made.

We want a real and lasting fix to the entire land into trust process. In our view, an amendment to the 1934 Indian Reorganization Act that extends tribal trust land acquisition authority to the Secretary of Interior must also include clear direction to provide adequate notice to local governments, ensure that local governments are consulted throughout the fee to trust process, provide incentives for tribes and local governments to work together. We want to do that. And provide for cooperating agreements that are enforceable.

Rather than authorize the Department to continue business as usual, this Committee should advance legislation that balances the legitimate interests of both tribal and county governments.

In closing, I ask you to note that CSAC has submitted formal written testimony for the record that includes additional details, more than I can give in this allotted oral time. One-fifth of the Nation's federally recognized tribes are in California. There are 352 applications for Federal recognition pending nationwide; one-fourth are from California.

If *Carcieri* reform occurs without addressing fee to trust reform, it will have a disproportionate impact on California compared to the rest of the Nation, because of the large numbers of tribes that could be positioned for trust land acquisition. I believe personally that that is why Senator Feinstein is so concerned about this issue.

The fee to trust process mus be part of a *Carcieri* fix. You will only fix part of the problem if you don't address the whole underlying situation. We need to look at this comprehensively. We urge you to work with counties to ensure that this historic opportunity is not missed.

Thank you very much.

[The prepared statement of Ms. Dillon follows:]

PREPARED STATEMENT OF DIANE DILLON, SUPERVISOR, NAPA COUNTY BOARD OF SUPERVISORS; MEMBER, CALIFORNIA STATE ASSOCIATION OF COUNTIES

Thank you Chairwoman Cantwell, Ranking Member Barrasso, and Members of the Committee for the opportunity to testify today. My name is Diane Dillon, and I am a County Supervisor in Napa County, California and am actively involved in the California State Association of Counties (CSAC). This testimony is submitted on behalf of CSAC, which has been actively engaged in pursuing federal laws and regulations that provide the framework for constructive government-to-government relationships between counties and tribes.

CSAC, which was founded in 1895, is the unified voice on behalf of all 58 of California's counties. The primary purpose of the association is to represent county government before the California Legislature, administrative agencies, and the federal government. CSAC places a strong emphasis on educating the public about the value and need for county programs and services.

The intent of this testimony is to provide a perspective from counties regarding the significance of the Supreme Court's decision in *Carcieri v. Salazar* and to recommend measures for the Committee to consider as it seeks to address the implications of the decision. The views presented herein also reflect policy positions of many State Attorneys General who are committed to the creation of a fee-to-trust process in which tribal interests can be met and legitimate state and local interests are properly considered.

In our view, the recent Carcieri decision provides Congress with a rare opportunity to address long-standing defects in the land-into-trust system. The current process—as authorized under the *Indian Reorganization Act of 1934* (IRA) and governed by the Department of the Interior's Part 151 regulations—lacks adequate standards and has led to significant, and in many cases, unnecessary conflict and distrust of the federal decisionmaking system for trust lands. It is from this local government experience regarding the fee-to-trust process that we address the implications of the *Carcieri* decision.

The Deficiencies of the Current Trust-Land Process

The fundamental problem with the trust acquisition process is that Congress has not set standards under which any delegated trust land authority would be applied by the Bureau of Indian Affairs (BIA). The relevant section of federal law, Section 5 of the IRA, reads as follows: "The Secretary of the Interior is hereby authorized in his discretion, to acquire [by various means] any interest in lands, water rights, or surface rights to lands, within or without reservations . . . for the purpose of providing land to Indians." 25 U.S.C. § 465.

The aforementioned general and undefined congressional guidance has resulted in a trust land process that fails to meaningfully include legitimate interests, provide adequate transparency to the public, or demonstrate fundamental balance in trust land decisions. The unsatisfactory process has created significant controversy, serious conflicts between tribes and states, counties and local governments—including litigation costly to all parties—and broad distrust of the fairness of the system.

It should be noted that the deficiencies in the trust land process were reaffirmed recently in a quantitative analysis of all 111 fee-to-trust decisions by the Pacific Region BIA Office between 2001 and 2011.[1] The analysis found that BIA granted 100 percent of the proposed acquisition requests and in no case did any Section 151 factor weigh against approval of an application.[2] The analysis further found that because of the lack of clear guidance and objective criteria, Pacific Region BIA decisions avoid substantive analysis in favor of filler considerations and boilerplate language.[3] The result is a broken process in which community concerns are ignored or downplayed, applications are rubber-stamped at a 100 percent acceptance rate, and tribes and local governments are forced into unnecessary and unproductive conflict.[4] The problem appears likely to worsen in the future, given recent statements by the Department trumpeting its desire to "keep that freight train moving" and "keep restoring lands for tribes."[5]

While there are a number of major flaws in BIA's fee-to-trust process, one of CSAC's central concerns is the severely limited role that state and local governments play. The implications of losing jurisdiction over local lands are very significant, including the loss of tax base, loss of planning and zoning authority, and the loss of environmental and other regulatory power. Yet, state, county and local governments are afforded limited, and often late, notice of a pending trust land application, and, under the current regulations, are asked to provide comments on two narrow issues only: (1) potential jurisdictional conflicts; and, (2) loss of tax revenues.

Moreover, the notice that local governments receive typically does not include the actual fee-to-trust application and often does not indicate how the applicant tribe intends to use the land. Further, in some cases, tribes have proposed a trust acquisition without identifying a use for the land; in other cases, tribes have identified a non-intensive, mundane use, only to change the use to heavy economic development, such as gaming or energy projects, soon after the land is acquired in trust.

Local governments also are often forced to resort to Freedom of Information Act (FOIA) requests to ascertain if a petition for an Indian lands determination—a key step in the process for a parcel of land to qualify for gaming—has been filed in their jurisdiction. Because many tribal land acquisitions ultimately will be used for economic development purposes—including gaming activities—there are often signifi-

---

[1] (Kelsey J. Waples, *Extreme Rubber Stamping: The Fee-to-Trust Process of the Indian Reorganization Act of 1934*, 40 Pepperdine Law Review 250 (2013).
[2] Id., pp. 278.
[3] Id., pp. 286, 293, 302.
[4] Id., pp. 292, 295, 297.
[5] See "Washburn Announces Plan of Attack for Patchak Plan," *http://indiancountrytodaymedianetwork.com/2013/05/24/washburn-announces-plan-attack-patchak-patch-149514.*

cant unmitigated impacts to the surrounding community, including environmental and economic impacts. Unfortunately, current law does not provide any incentive for tribes and affected local governments to enter into agreements for the mitigation of off-reservation impacts.

While the Department of the Interior understands the increased impacts and conflicts inherent in recent trust land decisions, it has not crafted regulations that strike a reasonable balance between tribes seeking new trust lands and the states and local governments experiencing unacceptable impacts. Indeed, the current notification process embodied in the Part 151 regulations is, in practice, insufficient and falls far short of providing local governments with the level of detail needed to adequately respond to proposed trust land acquisitions. Accordingly, a legislative effort is needed to meet the fundamental interests of both tribes and local governments.

Carcieri v. Salazar—An Historic Opportunity

On February 24, 2009, the U.S. Supreme Court issued its landmark decision on Indian trust lands in Carcieri v. Salazar. The Court held that the Secretary of the Interior lacks authority to take land into trust on behalf of Indian tribes that were not under the jurisdiction of the Federal Government upon enactment of the IRA in 1934.

Because the *Carcieri* decision has definitively confirmed the Secretary's lack of authority to take land into trust for post-1934 tribes, Congress has the opportunity not just to address the issue of the Secretary's authority under the current failed fee-to-trust system, but to reassert its primary authority for these decisions by setting specific standards for taking land into trust that address the main shortcomings of the trust land process.

In the wake of this significant court decision, varied proposals for reversing the *Carcieri* decision have been generated, some proposing administrative action and others favoring a congressional approach. Today's hearing, like several hearings before it, is a recognition of the significance of the *Carcieri* decision and the need to consider legislative action.

We believe that the responsibility to address the implications of *Carcieri* clearly rests with Congress and that a decision to do so in isolation of the larger problems of the fee-to-trust system would represent an historic missed opportunity. Indeed, a legislative resolution that hastily returns the trust land system to its status before *Carcieri* will be regarded as unsatisfactory to counties, local governments, and the people we serve. Rather than a "fix," such a result would only perpetuate a broken system, where the non-tribal entities most affected by the trust acquisition process are without a meaningful role. Ultimately, this would undermine the respectful government-to-government relationship that is necessary for both tribes and neighboring governments to fully develop, thrive, and serve the people dependent upon them for their well being.

Our primary recommendation to the Committee and to Congress is this: Do not advance a congressional response to *Carcieri* that allows the Secretary of the Interior to return to the flawed fee-to-trust process. Rather, Congress should make meaningful, comprehensive reforms to the trust land system. Legislation should include provisions that ensure local governments and impacted parties are able to file a challenge to a trust acquisition decision before title to the land is transferred. Such a change is necessary in light of the Department of the Interior's recent decision—discussed in further detail below—to eliminate the waiting period in which the Secretary was required to publish a notice of a trust decision 30 days before actually acquiring title to the land.

CSAC believes that the *Carcieri* decision presents Congress with an opportunity to carefully exercise its constitutional authority for fee-to-trust acquisitions and to define the respective roles of Congress and the Executive Branch in trust land decisions. Additionally, it affords Congress with the opportunity to establish clear and specific congressional standards and processes to guide trust land decisions in the future. A clear definition of roles is acutely needed regardless of whether trust and recognition decisions are ultimately made by Congress, as provided in the Constitution, or the Executive Branch under a congressional grant of authority.

It should be noted that Congress has the power to not provide new standard-less authority to the Executive Branch for trust land decisions and instead retain its own authority to make these decisions on a case-by-case basis as it has done in the past, although decreasingly in recent years. Whether or not Congress chooses to retain its authority or to delegate it in some way, it owes it to tribes and to states, counties, local governments and communities, to provide clear direction to the Secretary of the Interior to make trust land decisions according to specific congressional standards and to eliminate much of the conflict inherent in such decisions under present practice.

Looking ahead, we respectfully urge Members of this Committee to consider a comprehensive approach to the problem in any legislation seeking to address the trust land process post-*Carcieri*, namely: (1) the absence of authority to acquire trust lands, which affects post-1934 tribes, and (2) the lack of meaningful standards and a fair and open process, which affects states, local governments, businesses and non-tribal communities. As Congress considers the trust land issue, it should undertake reform that is in the interests of all affected parties.

Some of the more important new standards should be as follows:

Notice and Transparency

1) *Require Full Disclosure from the Tribes on Trust Land Applications and Other Indian Land Decisions, and Fair Notice and Transparency from the BIA.* The Part 151 regulations are not specific and do not require sufficient information about tribal plans to use the land proposed for trust status. As a result, it is very difficult for affected parties (local and state governments, and the public) to determine the nature of the tribal proposal, evaluate the impacts, and provide meaningful comments.

BIA should be directed to require tribes to provide reasonably detailed information to state and affected local governments, as well as the public, about the proposed uses of the land early on, not unlike the public information required for planning, zoning and permitting on the local level. This assumes even greater importance since local planning, zoning and permitting are being preempted by the trust land decision; accordingly, information about intended uses is reasonable and fair to require.

Legislative and regulatory changes need to be made to ensure that affected governments receive timely notice of fee-to-trust applications and petitions for Indian land determinations in their jurisdiction and have adequate time to provide meaningful input. Indian lands determinations, a critical step for a tribe to take land into trust for gaming purposes, is conducted in secret without notice to affected counties or any real opportunity for input. As previously indicated, counties are often forced to file a FOIA request to even determine if an application was filed and the basis for the petition.

Notice for trust and other land actions for tribes that go to counties and other governments is not only very limited in coverage, the opportunity to comment is minimal; this must change. A new paradigm is needed where counties are considered meaningful and constructive stakeholders in Indian land-related determinations. For too long, counties have been excluded from providing input in critical Department of Interior decisions and policy formation that directly affects their communities. This remains true today as evidenced by new policies being announced by the Administration without input from or consultation with local government organizations.

The corollary is that consultation with counties and local governments must be substantive, include all affected communities, and provide an opportunity for public comment. Under Part 151, BIA does not invite comment by third parties even though they may experience major negative impacts, although it will accept and review such comments. BIA accepts comments only from the affected state and the local government with legal jurisdiction over the land and, from those parties, only on the narrow question of tax revenue loss, government services currently provided to the subject parcels, and zoning conflicts. As a result, under current BIA practice, trust acquisition requests are reviewed under a very one-sided and incomplete record that does not provide real consultation or an adequate representation of the consequences of the decision. Broad notice of trust applications should be required with at least 90 days to respond.

Define Tribal Need

2) *The BIA Should Define ''Tribal Need'' and Require Specific Information about Need from the Tribes.* The BIA regulations provide inadequate guidance as to what constitutes legitimate tribal need for a trust land acquisition. There are no standards other than the stipulation that the land is necessary to facilitate tribal self-determination, economic development or Indian housing. These standards can be met by virtually any trust land request, regardless of how successful the tribe is or how much land it already owns. As a result, there are numerous examples of BIA taking additional land into trust for economically and governmentally self-sufficient tribes already having wealth and large land bases.

Congress should consider developing standards requiring justification of the need and purpose for acquisition of additional trust lands so that the acquisition process does not continue to be a ''blank check'' for removing land from state and local jurisdiction. Notably, CSAC supports a lower threshold for acquisition of trust land that will be used only for non-gaming or non-intensive economic purposes, including governmental uses and housing projects.

Changes in Use of Land

3) *Applications Should Require Specific Representations of Intended Uses.* Changes in use should not be permitted without further reviews, including environmental impacts, and application of relevant procedures and limitations. Such further review should have the same notice, comment, and consultation as the initial application. The law also should be changed to explicitly authorize restrictions and conditions to be placed on land going into trust that further the interests of both affected tribes and other affected governments.

Intergovernmental Agreements

4) *Tribes that Reach Local Intergovernmental Agreements to Address Jurisdiction and Environmental Impacts Should Have a Streamlined Process.* The legal framework should encourage tribes to reach intergovernmental agreements to address off-reservation project impacts by reducing the threshold for demonstrating need when such agreements are in place. Tribes, states, and counties need a process that is less costly and more efficient. The virtually unfettered discretion contained in the current process, due to the lack of clear standards, almost inevitably creates conflict and burdens the system. A process that encourages cooperation and communication provides a basis to expedite decisions and reduce costs and frustration for all involved.

It should be noted that an approach that encourages intergovernmental agreements between a tribe and local government affected by fee-to-trust applications is required and working well under recent California State gaming compacts. Not only does such an approach offer the opportunity to streamline the application process, it can also help to ensure the success of the tribal project within the local community. The establishment of a trust land system that incentivizes intergovernmental agreements between tribes and local governments is at the heart of CSAC's fee-to-trust reform recommendations and should be a top priority for Congress.

Clear and Objective Standards

5) *Establish Clear and Objective Standards for Agency Exercise of Discretion in Making Fee-to-Trust Decisions.* The lack of meaningful standards or any objective criteria in fee-to-trust decisions made by the BIA have been long criticized by the U.S. Government Accountability Office and local governments. For example, BIA requests only minimal information about the impacts of such acquisitions on local communities and trust land decisions are not governed by a requirement to balance the benefit to the tribe against the impact to the local community. As a result, there are well-known and significant impacts of trust land decisions on communities and states, with consequent controversy and delay and distrust of the process.

Furthermore, the BIA has the specific mission to serve Indians and tribes and is granted broad discretion to decide in favor of tribes. In order to reasonably balance the interests of tribes and local governments, the Executive Branch should be given clear direction from Congress regarding considerations of need and mitigation of impacts to approve a trust land acquisition. However any delegation of authority is resolved, Congress must specifically direct clear and balanced standards that ensure that trust land requests cannot be approved where the negative impacts to other parties outweigh the benefit to the tribe.

The attached fee-to-trust legislative reform proposal developed by CSAC seeks to address the inequities and flaws in the current trust land system. The centerpiece of the reform package is a proposal that would provide an incentive for tribes and local governments to enter into judicially enforceable mitigation agreements. Additionally, the proposal would remedy the serious defects in the fee-to-trust process related to inadequate notification and consultation requirements, including those outlined in the aforementioned *Pepperdine Law Review* analysis of fee-to-trust decisions, as well as address other significant shortcomings in the trust land system.

Appeals of Land Acquisition Decisions

On November 13th of this year, the Department of the Interior finalized a new rule governing decisions by the Secretary to approve or deny applications to acquire land in trust. CSAC believes that the final rule, which amends the Department's 151 regulations, will expedite trust approvals to the detriment of all interested parties, and to the administrative process itself.

The rule (found at *25 CFR Part 151, BIA–2013–0005, RIN 1076–AF15*) effectively repeals the Department's ''self-stay'' policy, which required the Secretary to publish a notice of a trust decision 30 days before actually transferring title. The now-eliminated waiting period was intended to ensure that interested parties had the opportunity to seek judicial review under the Administrative Procedure Act (APA) before the Secretary acquired title to land in trust. In virtually all past cases, if a challenger filed suit within the 30-day window, the Secretary agreed to "self-stay" the trust transfer during court proceedings, thus allowing for the orderly resolution of the challenge.

It should be noted that the Department's new rule incorrectly asserts that because of the Supreme Court's 2012 decision in *Match-E-Be-Nash-She-Wish Band of Pottawatomi Indians v. Patchak*, eliminating the current 30-day wait period will not effect a change in the law or affect any parties' rights under current law. In *Patchak*, the Court determined that the Quiet Title Act did not bar APA challenges to trust decisions after title transfer to the United States. However, as described below, the final rule puts local governments in a far worse position by dramatically altering the balance of equities and eliminating their ability to obtain emergency relief after a decision to accept the land in trust, but before the land achieves trust status.

The rule fails to recognize that the facts on the ground and balance of equities changes when land achieves trust status and development commences. The rule directs the Secretary or other BIA official to "immediately acquire the land in trust" after a decision becomes final, and the BIA is encouraging tribes to begin development immediately upon acceptance of land into trust. Both of these steps appear intended to foreclose concerned parties from obtaining emergency relief, even with regard to trust decisions that are clearly inappropriate and arbitrary. Courts are less likely to order emergency relief if a tribe and its development partners have invested resources and substantially implemented a gaming or other development project. Indeed, courts may be unable to grant relief at all if tribes decline to participate in the action and claim sovereign immunity.

The rule also contravenes protections in the APA for parties seeking emergency relief from administrative decisions. In particular, Section 705 of the APA authorizes federal courts to postpone the effective date of an agency action and to preserve status or rights pending conclusion of the review proceedings. The rule circumvents Section 705 by pushing land transfers before an affected party can seek judicial review and allow the courts to exercise their authority to review trust transfers. Communities and local governments will be harmed because, even if successful in the litigation, their success likely will not bring back the tax revenue and other fees lost when the land went into trust, nor remove the incompatible developments that are not permitted under comprehensive local land use plans, now possible without the rule.

The Department's push for immediate project implementation also appears intended to impede a court's ability to award complete relief. Litigation can take years to reach a final decision, which raises strong concerns regarding the Department's practical ability to unwind a trust decision and remove land from trust. The rule ignores these concerns, and includes no procedure for undoing a trust decision in a transparent and orderly manner.

The Department is amiss in asserting that these harms are balanced by the rule's requirements regarding the notification of decisions and administrative appeal rights. These changes are equally flawed, as the rule requires communities and local governments to make themselves known to BIA officials at every decisionmaking level to receive written notice of a trust land acquisition. It will be extremely difficult for anyone to sort through local and national BIA organizational charts to try to determine how, when, and by whom a particular application will be processed. BIA decisionmaking is far from transparent today, and the rule will make the process even more opaque and participation more difficult in the future.

In light of the Department's new rule, we believe that Congress should seek legislative changes that would entitle a party, upon timely request, to an automatic 30 day stay of a decision approving a trust application. A stay of decision should hold true whether a party has appealed a trust decision to the Interior Board of Indian Appeals, or has appeared before the Assistant Secretary—Indian Affairs. This would enable the party to preserve its rights by seeking a judicial order staying the effectiveness of any Departmental approval pending the court's review of the validity of that decision.

Additional provisions requiring BIA to publish trust applications on its website, provide regular updates as to the status of its review, identify the decision-makers responsible for an application, and provide contact information to allow parties to identify themselves as interested parties also should be required. Parties should be exempt from exhaustion requirements in the absence of substantial compliance with these provisions.

California's Situation and the Need for a Suspension of Fee-To-Trust Application Processing

California's unique cultural history and geography, and the fact that there are over 100 federally-recognized tribes in the state, contributes to the fact that no two fee-to-trust applications are alike. The diversity of applications and circumstances in California reinforce the need for both clear, objective standards in the fee-to-trust process and the importance of local intergovernmental agreements to address particular concerns.

The sheer number of pending applications in California further amplifies the need for reform. From 2011 to September of 2013 alone, dozens of California tribes submitted fee-to-trust applications—for both gaming and non-gaming purposes—totaling more than 9,600 acres of land. Numerous previously submitted applications remain in process at the Department of the Interior representing tens of thousands of additional acres of land that could be removed from state and federal tax rolls and exempt from county and state regulatory control.

The Supreme Court's decision in *Carcieri* complicates the picture in California and across the country. As previously discussed, the Court held that the authority of the Secretary of the Interior to take land into trust for tribes extends only to those tribes under federal jurisdiction in 1934. However, the phrase ''under federal jurisdiction'' is not defined.

Notably, many California tribes are located on ''Rancherias,'' which were originally federal property on which homeless Indians were placed. No ''recognition'' was extended to most of these tribes at that time. If legislation to change the result in *Carcieri* is considered, it is essential that changes be made to the fee-to-trust processes to ensure improved notice to counties and to better define standards to remove property from local jurisdiction. Requirements must be established to ensure that the significant off-reservation impacts of tribal projects are fully mitigated. In particular, any new legislation should address the significant issues raised in states like California, which did not generally have a ''reservation'' system, and that are now faced with small Bands of tribal people who are recognized by the Federal Government as tribes and who are anxious to establish large commercial casinos.

In the meantime, CSAC strongly urges the Department of the Interior to suspend further fee-to-trust land acquisitions until Carcieri's implications are better understood and legislation is passed to better define when and which tribes may acquire land, particularly for gaming purposes.

Pending Legislation

As stated above, congressional action must address the critical repairs needed in the fee-to-trust process. Unfortunately, legislation currently pending in the House (H.R. 279 and H.R. 666) fails to set clear standards for taking land into trust, to properly balance the roles and interests of tribes, state, local and federal governments in these decisions, and to clearly address the apparent usurpation of authority by the Executive Branch over Congress' constitutional authority over tribal recognition.

H.R. 279, in particular, serves to expand the undelegated power of the Department of the Interior by expanding the definition of an Indian tribe under the IRA to any community the Secretary *''acknowledges* to exist as an Indian Tribe [emphasis added].'' In doing so, the effect of the bill is to facilitate off-reservation activities by tribes and perpetuate the inconsistent standards that have been used to create tribal entities. Such a ''solution'' causes controversy and conflict rather than an open process which, particularly in states such as California, is needed to address the varied circumstances of local governments and tribes.

Conclusion

We ask Members of the Committee to incorporate the aforementioned requests into any Congressional actions that may emerge regarding the *Carcieri* decision. Congress must take the lead in any legal repair for inequities caused by the Supreme Court's action, but absolutely should not do so without addressing these reforms. CSAC's proposals are common-sense reforms, based upon a broad national base of experience on these issues that, if enacted, will eliminate some of the most controversial and problematic elements of the current trust land acquisition process. The result would help states, local governments and non-tribal stakeholders. It also would assist trust land applicants by guiding their requests towards a collaborative process and, in doing so, reduce the delay and controversy that now routinely accompany acquisition requests.

We also urge Members to reject any ''one-size-fits-all'' solution to these issues. In our view, the Indian Gaming Regulatory Act has often represented such an approach, and as a result has caused many problems throughout the nation where the sheer number of tribal entities and the great disparity among them requires a thoughtful case-by-case analysis of each tribal land acquisition decision.

Thank you for considering these views.

Attachment

California State Association of Counties

COMPREHENSIVE FEE-TO-TRUST REFORM PROPOSAL

1100 K Street
Suite 101
Sacramento
California
95814

telephone
916.327-7500
facsimile
916.441.5507

Section 5 of the Indian Reorganization Act, 25 U.S.C. § 465

The Secretary of the Interior is authorized, in his discretion, to acquire, through purchase, relinquishment, gift, exchange, or assignment, any interest in lands, water rights, or surface rights to lands, within or without existing reservations, including trust or otherwise restricted allotments, whether the allottee be living or deceased, for the purpose of providing land for Indians.

For the acquisition of such lands, interests in lands, water rights, and surface rights, and for expenses incident to such acquisition, there is authorized to be appropriated, out of any funds in the Treasury not otherwise appropriated, a sum not to exceed $2,000,000 in any one fiscal year: Provided, that no part of such funds shall be used to acquire additional land outside of the exterior boundaries of Navajo Indian Reservation for the Navajo Indians in Arizona, nor in New Mexico, in the event that legislation to define the exterior boundaries of the Navajo Indian Reservation in New Mexico, and for other purposes, or similar legislation, becomes law.

The unexpended balances of any appropriations made pursuant to this section shall remain available until expended.

Title to any lands or rights acquired pursuant to this Act or the Act of July 28, 1955 (69 Stat. 392), as amended (25 U.S.C. 608 et seq.) shall be taken in the name of the United States in trust for the Indian tribe or individual Indian for which the land is acquired, and such lands or rights shall be exempt from State and local taxation.

The Secretary may acquire land in trust pursuant to this section where the applicant has identified a specific use of the land and:

(a)   the Indian tribe or individual Indian applicant has executed enforceable agreements with each jurisdictional local government addressing the impacts of the proposed trust acquisition; or

(b)   In the absence of the agreements identified in subsection (a):

    (1)   the Indian tribe or individual Indian demonstrates, and the Secretary determines, that:

        (A)   the land will be used for non-economic purposes, including for religious, cultural, tribal housing, or governmental facilities, and the applicant lacks sufficient trust land for that purpose; or

        (B)   the land will be used for economic or gaming purposes and the applicant has not achieved economic self-sufficiency and lacks sufficient trust land for that purpose;

    and

(2)   the Secretary determines, after consulting with appropriate state and local officials, that the acquisition would not be detrimental to the surrounding community and that all significant jurisdictional conflicts and impacts, including increased costs of services, lost revenues, and environmental impacts, have been mitigated to the extent practicable.

(c)   notice and a copy of any application, partial or complete, to have land acquired in trust shall be provided by the Secretary to the State and affected local government units within twenty (20) days of receipt of the application, or of any supplement to it. The Secretary shall provide affected local governmental units at least ninety (90) days to submit comments from receipt of notice and a copy of the complete application to have land acquired in trust.

(d)   a material change in use of existing tribal trust land that significantly increases impacts, including gaming or gaming-related uses, shall require approval of the Secretary under this section, and satisfy the requirements of the National Environmental Policy Act, 42 U.S.C. § 4321 et seq., and, if applicable, the Indian Gaming Regulatory Act, 25 U.S.C. § 2701 et seq.;

(1)   the Secretary shall notify the State and affected local government units within twenty (20) days of any change in use in trust land initiated by an applicant under this subsection.

(2)   as soon as practicable following any change in use in trust land initiated prior to review and approval under this section, the Secretary shall take steps to stop the new use, including suit in federal court, upon application by an affected local government;

(3)   any person may file an action under 5 U.S.C. § 701 et seq. to compel the Secretary to enjoin any change in use in trust land initiated prior to review and approval under this section.

(e)   notwithstanding any other provisions of law, the Secretary is authorized to include restrictions on use in the deed transferred to the United States to hold land in trust for the benefit of the Indian tribe or individual Indian and shall consider restricting use in cases involving significant jurisdictional and land use conflicts upon application of governments having jurisdiction over the land;

(f)   any agreement executed pursuant to subsection (a) of this section shall be deemed approved by the Secretary and enforceable according to the terms of the agreement upon acquisition in trust of land by the Secretary;

(g)   the Secretary shall promulgate regulations implementing these amendments within 365 days of enactment.

The CHAIRWOMAN. Thank you, and thank you for your testimony
I think I might just start with you on a couple of things. One, do you know if the counties took any position or had any position prior to the gaming laws that were on the books? Did the counties ever have problems in dealing with land into trust issues or take a formal position?

Ms. DILLON. You mean prior to 1988?

The CHAIRWOMAN. Yes.

Ms. DILLON. I don't know that. I don't know that. And I don't have a lot of specific details at hand. I was only informed about this hearing a week ago Friday. And we were not able to compile all that we would like to present. I understand we have another two weeks to present that.

The CHAIRWOMAN. Yes. Do you think any of the current issues that your county association, just within California, and we will submit the NACO letter for the record, but on your California counties, do you think there are any issues that they have in taking land into trust that aren't related to gaming?

Ms. DILLON. Oh, yes, I would definitely say so. As you know, California produces one-third of the Nation's food crop. We have a very great concern about diminishing agricultural land. In California in the 1940s, 1950s and 1960s and into the 1970s, we saw subdivisions encroach on agricultural land. But in the last 20 to 30 years, there has been a concentrated focus on protecting agricultural land and not having sprawl, as we saw in that period of time.

We are working, for instance, in my county, very closely with the Napa Valley Vintners Association, because counties do not have the ability to engage and there is no, there is not an approach with this process that encourages local cooperative agreements, we have no real protection in terms of anyone who acquires or a tribal entity, for instance, that acquires agricultural land, in keeping it in agriculture, in making sure that that is how it continues, and in making sure that other issues concerning water use and so forth are adhered to.

Without that enforceability mechanism, we have great concerns, even with regard to lands taken into trust for agricultural purposes.

The CHAIRWOMAN. So do you know if any of the California counties have ever objected or sent remarks, testimony, to the Department of Interior on a project that is not gaming?

Ms. DILLON. I don't know that personally, but I intend to find out.

The CHAIRWOMAN. That would be great, thank you. I am just curious to know and understand on that.

And has your association taken a position on tribal sovereignty?

Ms. DILLON. I don't know that we have a formal position. I believe our written remarks, the written testimony reflects our great respect for tribal sovereignty. This is not the concern that we have. It is not our position that we want to have local control. We are simply advocating to be able to have cooperative agreements. That is not the path that California is headed in.

The CHAIRWOMAN. If I could turn to Ms. Johnson-Pata. I was asking the Assistant Secretary this issue about economic impact, because I feel like we have had this chilling effect and it is hard to understand or measure how much has been slowed down. Do you have any data from the National Congress of American Indians on that?

Ms. JOHNSON-PATA. I made a note of that when you were asking that question. The difficulty with that is, we hear the stories, I hear from tribes, several tribes who have let us know about investors who have decided not to invest because of the uncertainty of the land. So we hear those stories, but those are really difficult for them to document. First of all, a tribe doesn't want to be in a position where maybe a future investor might be a little concerned. And secondly, investors don't want to be seen as red-lining. So that becomes one of the challenges, I think, in doing so.

When you asked that question, I was thinking if there was a possible way for us to do some kind of confidential kind of survey to get some kind of grasp of economic impact. But I will check with our folks at the Policy Research Center to see if there is a means of being able to come up with that. It is pretty targeted right now with the 18 cases that are moving forward. Certainly cases adjacent to those areas would probably be more targeted.

But overall, I don't know how you measure the economic impact of slow decision-making, which I think is the most critical right now. Decision-making around particularly energy development and lands that would be utilized for energy development and the slowed process of taking land into trust and to addressing those decisions has increased, created a bottleneck for tribal development moving forward. That causes a chilling effect on investors and folks who want to have some co-development responsibilities with tribes.

The CHAIRWOMAN. To me, it is an important issue. I know, as you say, it is probably hard to document. We could probably look at pre-2009 and see what the average permit process was.

Ms. JOHNSON-PATA. The time line.

The CHAIRWOMAN. Time line, even excluding gaming. But again, the reason I mention this is because I think most of my colleagues think this issue has to deal with land into trust, when in reality I think it probably deals more with NIGRA and the process by which tribes are recognized. Those two issues, as opposed to really the land into trust issue. Land into trust is just the last step in a process.

Ms. JOHNSON-PATA. Right.

The CHAIRWOMAN. As opposed to, we have many previous chairs to me who have had many, many hearings on the failure to implement various policies after the original Gaming Act was implemented, and then the policy decisions to follow on that. A lot of those got dragged out over a long period of time and caused lots of challenges and things that we are still dealing with.

But I think it is interesting that we don't have any data to measure this. Maybe that is why most of my colleagues think this issue deals with gaming, when 98 percent of it doesn't have anything to do with gaming.

Ms. JOHNSON-PATA. We will definitely work on a report that we can at least share with you, as much as we are able, to quantitatively put together.

The CHAIRWOMAN. Okay. And what would you say is certainty in the process? What do you think is a time frame for, what kind of process for reviewing land into trust and getting land through a process, what do you think certainty is?

Ms. JOHNSON-PATA. Prior to *Patchak*, we got, the certainty was once the Department made a determination, that that was the determination the tribe could move forward. And that was really critically important for us, because we believe our relationship is with the Federal Government. And when the Federal Government makes this decision that says, this land is taken into trust for the purpose of the tribe to develop or to do what it is intended to do, that should be certainty. And it shouldn't be second-guessed again.

So I believe that that is what certainty is. We have worked with the Department to try to make sure that we can at least identify any folks that may have challenges to the taking of that land into trust, so that there is a process for addressing that. So the uncertainty of who may be out there in the world of challenges is limited. So certainty is, I believe, when the Department takes that action and finalizes that action, that should be what certainty is.

The CHAIRWOMAN. You don't have a time frame in mind?

Ms. JOHNSON-PATA. A time frame?

The CHAIRWOMAN. Well, just in the sense of, I guess on all these, we have hydro relicensing that happens every 50 years. I think it takes probably about 10 years to decide the relicensing of hydro. Some people would say, in a very appropriate need, because hydro relicensing has to balance a lot of different needs, a lot of people have to weigh in, a lot of people have to discuss. I think my former colleague from Idaho and I worked on a process to make that a little smoother. Because 10 years is a pretty long time to go through a process.

Ms. JOHNSON-PATA. And unfortunately, some of these land into trust applications are 10 years plus. Because as they are having to deal with some of the nuances, every single application is different. And there are things to be able to consider. That is why I think that trying to develop, the regulatory process allows for that engagement, to evaluate those applications on a case by case basis. And I would be concerned about legislation that so narrowly constrained this conversation about even ancestral land, for example. The stories were different for each tribe. I think that is important.

The current process, the pre-*Patchak* process was that the Department made that decision, and then there was that 30 days and it was final, that was it. Thirty days for comments and then it was final. Now today, they make a decision and we note who potentially has challenges. And then we weigh out their ability to decide whether or not they want to litigate. And we know at least what the scope of that will be.

I think reasonable time frames, like in any process, if someone was, housing for example, something I know more about, a tribe purchases a parcel for housing. And clearly, like any other development, you should reasonable think that within three months to six months at max, you should be able to finalize and close your loan, right? That process doesn't happen. And it has become more labored because of the longer term of all these questions that have to go about, rather than just looking at this as a parcel of land, as being brought to the tribe to provide housing to its people as you would purchase housing as a developer or somebody else would purchase housing in the common market.

The CHAIRWOMAN. Senator Begich?

Senator BEGICH. Thank you very much.

Jackie, let me ask you a question, I don't know if you can answer this, and again, I don't come from a State that has gaming. And I agree with the Chairwoman, it seems like that is all this issue continues to circle around, but really it is a very small percentage. But let me ask you, in California, I am going to use California as an example, aren't there compacts with the State in regard to the arrangement?

Ms. JOHNSON-PATA. There is.

Senator BEGICH. And there are financial arrangements, right?

Ms. JOHNSON-PATA. Yes, there is. Extensive compacts with the State, particularly in California.

Senator BEGICH. Right, but financial arrangements, too.

Ms. JOHNSON-PATA. Yes.

Senator BEGICH. So the State receives some of the proceeds?

Ms. JOHNSON-PATA. Most of the proceeds, each tribe negotiates their compact. But they have pretty much a standard in California.

Senator BEGICH. But it is a percentage?

Ms. JOHNSON-PATA. It is a range around 25 percent.

Senator BEGICH. Yes, so the State gets some money.

Ms. JOHNSON-PATA. Yes.

Senator BEGICH. My guess is they probably don't distribute it equally to the counties. That is a different problem. I know this from my State, which has oil wealth, that my State, they are cloudy sometimes on giving it to local governments. As a former mayor, I always believe the States shouldn't have the money, but that is a different issue.

So I am sensing, I am just guessing here that there are impacts, I don't deny that. Just like if a Wal-Mart opened up, there are going to be impacts. If they develop a mall, there are going to be impacts. There are always impacts. Matter of fact, most counties and cities, residential development, if you took it as an economic model, is a loser because of all the costs of services that go along with it, versus a commercial building and compacted lot that produces a lot of jobs and potential revenue, sales tax, especially in California. We don't have it in Anchorage.

But I want to make sure on that point

Ms. JOHNSON-PATA. Yes

Senator BEGICH. So let me, if I can, Ms Dillon, I am struggling with this, because I am sitting here, and it reminds me for a moment of city council time, when I was on the city council. Communities don't want certain things in the neighborhood. I will take LA County, we don't have counties, we have boroughs, but LA County, 30 some different cities work in that county. Each city tries to take business from each other. But one city doesn't regulate another city.

And this is the fundamental issue that I am struggling with here. Tribes have a government-to-government relationship. That is what they are. They are governments. We get a little foggy sometimes around here about what that means. But it is very clear to me. It is a government-to-government relationship. So it is no different than, I will use LA County, with 32 cities, when one city says, I am going to do X, and the city next door, I will use a city where I have an investment in, in Nevada, Carson City. Because Carson City wouldn't do the right deal with a developer, they went right over the city line and built a development there.

Of course, the city doesn't have the right to tell that city what to do. Because the city made a choice, the developer made a choice.

In this situation, I am struggling, when a tribe, a government, recognized by the Federal Government, decides to do something in their jurisdiction and rights, how that is different from a city next door who decides to do something that the city on the other side doesn't like. Help me understand that. Do you see what I am saying?

Ms. DILLON. I do.

Senator BEGICH. That is the fundamental issue here, it is a government-to-government relationship.

Ms. DILLON. It is a government-to-government relationship. And I can't speak to the other 49 States, obviously. But in California, we have something called LAFCO, Local Area Formation Commission, in every county, that includes the county and the cities in that county. They are not allowed, things that are inter-jurisdictional, of what the kind you are describing, where a city might acquire land in the county, that is not allowed to happen unless it goes through the LAFCO process.

So we all have to answer to something greater than ourselves.

Senator BEGICH. But the challenge is, we took their land. So they are trying to get their land back. It is different than a city. But that agreement you have doesn't tell a city that another city can veto what they want to do in their city, correct?

Ms. DILLON. No, and our concern is not, once, our issue isn't with tribal sovereignty.

Senator BEGICH. I get that. But they get their land, that is part of their government, what does that matter what they then do with it? It is similar to a city to city relationship.

Ms. DILLON. Our concerns are with that fee to trust process in terms of ancestral land, in terms of, is that the land that this Native American group had before, that they should now be able to reacquire and then deal with as they would desire. We are talking about way back early int eh process, about the acquisition of land.

And the fact of the matter is that in a place like California, despite the fact that we have vast areas that are open space and in national parks and Federal lands, 39 million of us, 80 percent of the 39 million are living in a pretty concentrated area. And what happens next door is very important and is affected. And we have, in the Bay Area where I live, we have 9 counties and 101 cities. And we work together to plan where housing goes. So we don't, yes, I can't tell Sonoma County or Solana County, my neighbors, what they can do. But we have gotten past that by working together on the bigger picture.

Senator BEGICH. But there is no jurisdictional requirements for you to do that. You just did it.

Ms. DILLON. Yes.

Senator BEGICH. I will tell you, every time I go to a community around the Country, I visit tribes, some landless tribes. Matter of fact, in the wine country, I was up north that they showed me some of their lands that they have been able to acquire that are ag lands. That was very impressive, that they were putting them into wine country land, in fact, to produce.

Ms. DILLON. Not in Napa County, but yes, that is right.

Senator BEGICH. Yes, Napa County is not only wine country, it is the wine country, I know in some people's minds, but it is not the only. I will tell you eastern Washington has some beautiful wine country. So it is all different.

But I am just saying to you that I saw the land. I thought it was very responsible. Because why? They were working with the local community. And it wasn't regulated for them to do that. It is good business and good for their community.

So that is why I understand your point of, let's try to catch everything. I am not seeing where the problem is at the level you are describing.

Now, I get where people don't like gaming. I get that. Our State does not allow gaming. The whole State. I get that. But this is only 1, 2 percent of the issue. I visit tribes all over the Country. And I will tell you, that is not the issue I see as the prevalent issue. I see people who have land that they want to get back into their homelands and then have a relationship with whatever those governments are adjoining them, and I have see it successful.

Now, does gaming by itself and its activity create all kinds of other activities? Yes. That is why in your State there is a compact or compacts, I should say, but if the State is not sharing that wealth and those impact dollars the right way, that is a different question that we can't answer here. I would love if I could figure out a way to tell my State that they need to give more money to local governments that they are taking on oil and gas revenues. They don't. They should, because that is the best expenditure location.

But I see multiple issues here. So I just want to kind of put it out there, not necessarily, I don't know if I need an answer. I am struggling with why this would not get the fix, get land going into trust again in the right way. And the cooperation I have seen in many communities I have visited is occurring without a regulatory process, without the Federal Government saying, you shall do this.

Ms. DILLON. If I might respond with three points, one is that probably, I am going to say, everybody in this room, we are all reasonable people. I bet we could all live in a town together and not even need zoning regulations. But that is not how the world works. We have to have laws for the 1 or 2 percent or however many there are that don't work cooperatively.

And I submit to you, I don't have actual names and places today, but I can tell you based on what I have heard from my colleagues in CSAC that there are, just as there are in every population, every group of folks, some folks who don't want to play by the rules, some folks who don't respect others. And that is why, respectfully, we are asking for a better regulatory structure. It doesn't have to do with the bulk of folks.

I also want to say that I agree that tribal nations deserve certainty. And I think in a government-to-government relationship both sides should have certainty. We need, county governments need to have certainty that the mitigations are addressed.

And I believe, I am not conversant on the law that creates the requirement for the compacts. But I will be looking into it, I can assure you, in the next two weeks.

Senator BEGICH. I bet you you should get your Governor to do a little revenue sharing off those compacts.

Ms. DILLON. Again, I have no idea if he is even allowed to. But I am going to, the last point I would like to make is with regard to the quantification that you are looking for. And the quantification that I see is the number of lawsuits. Any time you have a situation with the number of lawsuits that we have out there, all this litigation, there is something wrong. And that is the proof of it.

Most of those lawsuits are not with regard to only the *Carcieri* issue.

So as an elected person, and I would guess that you feel the same way, our job is to try to fix things so that future litigation doesn't occur. I think this Committee is in a place to be able to do that if more than the *Carcieri* fix is addressed.

The CHAIRWOMAN. I am sorry, did you say most of them were related? Did you mean most of those other issues weren't related to gaming or they were related to gaming? When you said most of these weren't related?

Ms. DILLON. I said the litigation that is out there is not all just related to *Carcieri* issues.

The CHAIRWOMAN. Meaning?

Ms. DILLON. It is related to fee to trust issues.

The CHAIRWOMAN. But mostly around gaming?

Ms. JOHNSON-PATA. They are fee to trust issues, but they are using the *Carcieri* as the their ability to pursue.

Ms. DILLON. And my point is, if I may, my point is simply by fixing *Carcieri* it is not going to make litigation go away. We had litigation before the *Carcieri* decision and I think we will continue to see it as long as the Department of Interior continues to operate with the interpretations. One of the things we have great concern about is the rule that was just adopted within the last two months. There hasn't been any litigation on it yet because it is not right. But I predict that we will be seeing some.

The CHAIRWOMAN. Well, as someone who chaired an energy subcommittee on water on the oversight of the San Joaquin water settlement issue, I agree. I think that had been like 18 years in litigation and finally everybody came to the table and said, this is what we want to do for water, which is basically figuring out how to more efficiently use the water in the Bay Area that people had. So I agree that it is a better process to figure out.

One of the things, I want to go back to Ms. Johnson-Pata, you heard Ms. Dillon, she says she doesn't want to affect tribal sovereignty. So one of the issues that I am interested in is if the association is encouraging a streamlined process, that is voluntary, do you think that impacts tribal sovereignty?

Ms. JOHNSON-PATA. A streamlined process that is voluntary?

The CHAIRWOMAN. Yes. One of the things, as I was mentioning earlier, the hydro relicensing decision, a lot of it was, people would wait in the process and then end up filing suit and it would elongate the process even longer. So one of the things that we did was say, you could form agreements up front. But they were voluntary. They were totally voluntary. It is just a way to get some of the issues on the table.

Ms. JOHNSON-PATA. I think you see that all the time with tribes. They choose to have cooperative agreements. I look at California, I have spent a great deal of time there. There are a lot of cooperative agreements in California with the local communities on the water, the fire protection, other issues that mitigate impacts. I think that tribes see that as being a good neighbor. I think Marshall speaks to that, being a good neighbor and providing resources outside of just their tribe in many ways.

So I think that is what we would all ultimately hope for, is to have those kinds of relationships.

The CHAIRWOMAN. Do those take place as part of a normal function on land into trust issues?

Ms. JOHNSON-PATA. It is very normal. It is part of a normal function.

The CHAIRWOMAN. So in the beginning of a land into trust, people would go and form, basically have a discussion with the local government?

Ms. JOHNSON-PATA. Every tribe who is pursuing land into trust ultimately wants to get to the land into trust. So if you are a businessman or tribal leader, you are going to take a look at what is out there as potential challenges and you are going to try to mitigate those or try to address them, try to be able to figure out how you can finalize your deal. And you don't go into it thinking that those things are going to become real obstacles. I don't know of any tribes who haven't tried to mitigate those issues. Challenges become when requests are unreasonable. And then all of a sudden, as happens in family groups, and other folks, those sometimes emotionally charged relationships then create their own obstacles to finding solutions together.

But I see agreements after agreements. In fact, at NCAI's website you can see, I think we have, we haven't done this for a while, but several years ago we went just to take a look at law enforcement agreements when we were getting ready for the TROA. And there were over 400 agreements between tribes and local governments, just on law enforcement alone, and cooperative agreements.

So Indian Country, it is a common use for us to be able to have agreements and to seek agreements with other governments in a respectful government-to-government relationship. Our point is, to make it very clear, our primary relationship is with the Federal Government. And this relationship with the Federal Government shouldn't be usurped by the county government. And we want to be able to make sure that when we make a decision with the Federal Government that that is a final decision. And that decision is what gets solidified through that relationship.

The CHAIRWOMAN. So a voluntary agreement, you are saying they are done and you would support voluntary agreements?

Ms. JOHNSON-PATA. Yes.

The CHAIRWOMAN. Okay. Mr. Chairman, do you have any input on the counties' recommendations for additional local level input?

Mr. PIERITE. Yes, Madam Chairwoman. When Tunica-Biloxi entered into the State compact negotiations with the State of Louisiana, we took a small contingency of community leaders with us. We agreed up front, they actually came with us and helped negotiate the State compact. We are looking at, we have entered tribal government agreement with them for social services to provide health service, mental health services, law enforcement services. So it has been done. We have been doing it for over 20 years.

And we always highly recommend that the counties or parish get involved with their tribal governments. Because it is the fair thing to do. And I want to echo what Ms. Johnson-Pata said, the trust responsibility, the relationship is between the tribal government and the U.S. government, not between the local counties and tribal governments. But we do respect our local governments and ask them into our reservation and work out any agreements for us to have a joint agreement.

Also I want to mention about Tunica-Biloxi has been working with the U.S. Chamber of Commerce. They have agreed to do a study on the impact of *Carcieri* as it relates to lack of economic development and job creation, because of *Carcieri*. Hopefully we will have that study within six months.

The CHAIRWOMAN. So when you were mentioning those compacts, those were compacts with the State of Louisiana around gaming issues?

Mr. PIERITE. The State of Louisiana, around gaming issues. We do have inter-tribal agreements as far as, inter-departmental agreements as far as law enforcement, mental health, social services. We just have a close working relationship with our community. I would strongly encourage all counties and parishes as well as Native American tribes, because you have to be good neighbors.

The CHAIRWOMAN. So if Tunica-Biloxi was taking land further into trust, would part of that at the beginning process be a dialogue with the local governments?

Mr. PIERITE. Yes. We would let them know that we were planning on putting land into trust and what is the purpose. Being good community partners allows respect to be built on both sides. One of the things about *Carcieri* is a lot of mis-communication being put out there as far as this being a gaming issue. This is not about gaming. This is about putting land into trust, about tribes to get back lands that they once owned and that were stolen from them. It is a spiritual connection to that land.

Before Columbus stumbled upon America, because he did not discover America, you cannot discover something where people were already here, Native Americans were here first. And all these lands were taken from us. I am not about to sit here and rehash old stuff, because we have to work together. You have to put it all in perspective and know that you have to be a good neighbor. But you have to be respectful of your neighbor. You have to respect their sovereignty. You have to respect what Native American Country has been through.

In my opening comments, I mentioned about Native Americans walked for centuries in darkness. You have to take that to heart. Sometimes you have to put your spiritual eyes on it and see what people have been through and see what it is all about. Once again, it is about a spiritual connection. Because in those same lands you are speaking of, there are some tribes there, used to own their land. And in them is burial grounds. And in those burial grounds is dreams that will never come into fruition, books that were never written, stories that never will be told, relationships that never will be formed. And you have to put all that into perspective.

It is not all about gaming. It is not all about dollars and sense. It is all about what we can bring back for our children, for our next generation. It is about securing the future for them. Thank you.

The CHAIRWOMAN. I don't think I ever failed to meet with you or be in your presence where you don't say something very profound and meaningful. Thank you for reminding us about all of that.

Are you saying on this notion of a streamlined process, if it was voluntary, if you are saying Tunica-Biloxi already do agreements, and you had a voluntary process and said, okay, you could have a streamlined process at Interior on land into trust if you had agreements, is that a problem? Is that acceptable?

Mr. PIERITE. My philosophy is, and I take difference with the demographic country philosophy, never enter, if you have the strength to enter into a conflict or confrontation, also into wisdom to bring resolution to same conflict or confrontation. So it is about sitting down to the table and discussing it. And yes, we will be willing to discuss it.

But one of the things about a clean *Carcieri* fix that I would like to go on record is, we don't want to leave any tribes behind. With a clean *Carcieri* fix, we want to make sure that each and every tribe has the ability to put land into trust. Because that is the only thing they can hold onto. That is the only thing they can reach out to. That is the only thing they can embrace.

The CHAIRWOMAN. I hear Ms. Dillon saying they just want to have some discussion. I hear other, there are all sorts of agreements going on or have gone on, there are other State ballot issues, I guess, or agreements, compacts that say okay, we don't want to be by schools or we don't want to be near this. So then I see Ms. Dillon, do you represent the Napa Valley area, is that what I heard?

Ms. DILLON. I am a county supervisor in Napa County, yes.

The CHAIRWOMAN. So I am assuming that one of these issues for you is you want to keep most of that land in wine production.

Ms. DILLON. We have the first agricultural preserve, our valley floor, in the United States, and that is our goal. We are the equivalent of Bordeaux, if you will. And it can't be replicated anywhere else.

The CHAIRWOMAN. And is that currently under threat by some proposed land into trust agreement?

Ms. DILLON. Not an actual land into trust, it hasn't reached that stage yet. There is a group seeking recognition through the Federal court system with the stated intention of acquiring land for a casino.

The CHAIRWOMAN. So is your issue with then their ability to be recognized and their holding, you said earlier you were not against tribal sovereignty, but you had questions about whether people had rights to access certain lands. I am trying to distinguish between
—

Ms. DILLON. We don't believe that the group of people who are seeking recognition necessarily have any connection with Napa County, that is more a desire to be in a relatively, well, a very well-known place that is highly desirable to many people as a place to be.

The CHAIRWOMAN. So I think some of those issues are in a different area of concern as it relates to Indian Country. I don't know, Ms. Johnson-Pata, whether you want to comment on that.

Ms. JOHNSON-PATA. I do. I think you hit it on the head. When there are, there are issues that are out there, folks that don't want something in their back yard, that comes up periodically in all kinds of development, inside and outside of Indian Country. We shouldn't clog up the system or for that matter, this whole Congressional process of trying to address land into trust, basic land into trust, pre-*Carcieri*, to make sure that we have the same rights that we had. All the Supreme Court was saying is, Congress, you need to clarify this.

I remember Chief Justice Breyer saying to us at NCAI, many years ago, he came to us and he said, there is some gray matter that is making it difficult in the courts. We need Congress to clarify. What we are saying to Congress is, we need you to clarify this so we can go back to having land brought into trust for all of these other beneficial reasons.

And this isn't the piece of legislation to piggyback on other issues and solutions. We want to be able to get back to pre-2009 status. And these other issues, such as Senator Begich talked about, I am from Alaska, this is a sensitive issue for me. But Alaska Natives have said, we want *Carcieri* for our brothers and sisters across the Country. We recognize our issue is tougher to deal with. We are not going to piggyback it onto the *Carcieri* fix. We are going to find another place for us to address that.

I say this is another issue that wasn't brought about by the challenge that this issue is. We can't use that as the vehicle to be all, fix all. But we certainly should have continued dialogue on this issue and find the appropriate vehicle to address other concerns that are clearly more of a local nature, that should not bottleneck the whole potential economic system of Indian Country when we are just barely beginning to rise up from where we have been and grasping economic opportunity.

And then now we can't develop our energy potential, we can't develop our reservation economies. Our health care facilities are stalled, our school systems are stalled, all because of this issue. This is not the vehicle to deal with an issue that has a controversy of a local nature that we can't fix in national legislation.

The CHAIRWOMAN. But you would say, Ms. Johnson-Pata, that the counties do deserve to have an opportunity to express their concerns about these kinds of issues, particularly as they come up in the process of who might get recognized and how they get recognized and the process of how they might then proceed.

Ms. JOHNSON-PATA. Absolutely. I think the process already says that people who have objections have a right to be able to voice their objections. And I think the process allows for that. I don't think those objections get elevated to the fact that every parcel of land that is being taken into trust for Indian Country should now be circumvented or stalled or a barrier to it, because somebody, and I am not just speaking to you, bu somebody has a concern in Napa Valley, so we want to change the whole system.

I think there should be a process to be able to have that kind of meaningful dialogue and solution oriented, but still recognize the ultimate authority is with the Federal Government and the tribes as they deal with their trust relationship that is constitutionally bound.

The CHAIRWOMAN. I did hear Ms. Dillon say that she wanted to honor that.

Ms. DILLON. I do.

The CHAIRWOMAN. I think that is good, and I hope you know what you mean when you say that. Those are big words, honoring and recognizing tribal sovereignty. There is a lot of law that goes with that.

Ms. DILLON. Let me say that you asked me about Napa County and I responded. But that is not why I am here. So I want to make that really clear. I am here representing CSAC, and that is 58 counties who have grave concerns, who have put forth a position paper of the changes that they would like to see Congress implement. And again, it is asking that there be incentives for tribes and local governments to work together and to provide for cooperating agreements that are enforceable.

If that is contrary to recognizing tribal sovereignty, then I will condition my prior statement. But what we would like to see is that as things evolve, we have a mechanism, an agreement for dealing with those issues, a working agreement. And as you know, California is a pretty heavily regulated State internally. We have new things coming up all the time that our State government wants us to do, with water, with wastewater, stormwater, constantly imposing new regulatory requirements that cost money.

Many of those require us to work on a watershed basis. If you will just let me give you an example. All of a sudden you will have a watershed area where the State makes a regulation and says, if 90 percent of the land in this watershed is not cooperating, then every landowner is going to have to pay on an individual basis to the State. So obviously it behooves everyone to work together in the watershed to minimize their costs on whatever particular regulation this was, for irrigated ag lands in this case.

But if we don't have a mechanism, if we had a tribal entity, for instance, that owned agricultural land and said, we are not going to participate, and we have no mechanism for enforcing that, it would have this impact that we would not be able to deal with, that was never anticipated at the time, perhaps, that the tribe acquired land.

So it is those kinds of issues, that is the kind of agreement that we need to have and would like to have on a local government to tribal government basis. That is just one example.

The CHAIRWOMAN. Okay. I thank all the witnesses. I have definitely pushed some things out there today in hopes that we might resolve this issue and move forward. I think I am in agreement with the panelists that if we end up in a legal lawsuit process that is just held up for years and years and years, that that is not going to be in our best interest, that we want to try and figure this out.

People have given good food for thought today about how to do that. And we will certainly be taking that into consideration as we think about legislative solutions.

I know how important this issue is to many people. We certainly want to restore, I think, what the 1934 Act had as an intention, which is not to divide tribes that are recognized. So we will be working on that issue and certainly taking into consideration how we move forward. But to do so that really brings about clarity.

And maybe that we have to do things that are clarifications in other areas, and just to get there. But certainly we want to move forward as soon as possible on clearing this up, so that this larger issue of taking land into trust that has just been such a historic part of what I think has been very positive self-governance for tribes, resulting in very positive economic development and in many cases very positive economic development for the entire region, continues and continue as it has in the past.

So we have a lot of work to do, but I thank all the witnesses for being here today and for their testimony.

Mr. PIERITE. Madam Chair, can I enter these letters of support from tribal leaders, tribal organization and community leaders into the record, please?

The CHAIRWOMAN. Without objection.

The CHAIRWOMAN. This hearing is adjourned.

[Whereupon, at 4:25 p.m., the Committee was adjourned.]

A P P E N D I X

PREPARED STATEMENT OF HON. WILLIAM IYALL, CHAIRMAN, COWLITZ INDIAN TRIBE

The Cowlitz Indian Tribe (''Cowlitz'' or ''Tribe'') is very appreciative of the Committee's commitment to resolving the crisis caused by the Supreme Court's decision in *Carcieri v. Salazar*, 555 U.S. 379 (2009), which has had devastating impacts on Indian Country—threatening tribal sovereignty and economic self-sufficiency, creating unequal treatment of federally-recognized Indian tribes contrary to Congressional intent, and resulting in costly, protracted litigation in which the United States is the defendant (at taxpayer expense). As I am sure you are aware, the Cowlitz Tribe is currently involved in just this type of litigation. As a result, Cowlitz is on the front line of the efforts to deal with the *Carcieri* decision and this experience has afforded us some valuable insight that we think might benefit the Committee in its consideration of this very important issue.

We greatly appreciate that the Committee held a hearing to address the issues raised by *Carcieri*. Cowlitz strongly believes that all federally recognized tribes should have equal access to the intended benefits of the Indian Reorganization Act (IRA), and that those benefits are crucial to ensuring that tribes have adequate trust lands on which to provide housing, education, health care, cultural and natural resource protection, economic development and governmental services to their members. But we are concerned about certain remarks made by some witnesses during the hearing suggesting changes that would effectively take the decision making out of the hands of the federal government and allow local governments to veto future trust acquisitions.

The IRA was enacted to effect a sea change in federal Indian policy, explicitly rejecting long-standing federal policies which had undermined the political and even physical existence of tribal nations. In particular, the IRA was meant to address the staggering loss of tribal land occasioned by passage of the General Allotment Act in 1887, which resulted in more than 90 million acres of tribal land passing out of trust status. The IRA provides a legal framework to support tribal governments and tribal economic development, and the most important component of that framework is the administrative mechanism to assist in the reacquisition of land for Indians. Any *Carcieri* fix must be viewed against this backdrop, and should not unduly or unfairly restrict the ability of Indian tribes to acquire trust lands.

Section 20 of the Indian Gaming Regulatory Act (IGRA) and the Department of the Interior's implementing regulations already include appropriate and extremely rigorous requirements that must be met before gaming can occur on Indian lands acquired in trust after October 17, 1988. Despite the concerns expressed by some witnesses during the hearing, approvals to acquire off-reservation lands for gaming are extremely rare. Indeed, the Cowlitz Tribe has been in the fee-to-trust process for more than eleven years now, and yet we still are landless. The notion that the Department is some kind of rubber stamp for new tribal casinos is almost comical to any tribe that actually has tried to go through the process. We do not believe that new restrictions are necessary, and we are concerned about incorporating new gaming-related requirements into a legislative vehicle aimed at addressing *Carcieri*.

The testimony from Senator Feinstein as well as Ms. Diane Dillon for the California State Association of Counties advocated for a greater role for local governments in the fee-to-trust process, focusing on gaming acquisitions.[1] She stated, ''I strongly believe that local governments must have the ability to influence the terms and conditions of the development of new casinos, especially because many communities simply do not want new casinos in their backyard.'' Ms. Dillon complained of the uncertainty for California counties with respect to planning caused by the creation of new Indian lands. But the fee-to-trust process already provides local govern-

[1] We note that Senator Feinstein's and Ms. Dillon's comments were focused entirely on Indian gaming rather than the fee-to-trust process. We must emphasize that these are two separate administrative processes, land acquisition being governed by the IRA and gaming eligibility by IGRA.

ments with ample opportunity to influence the terms and conditions of the Secretary's decision. 25 C.F.R. Part 151 specifically provides for State and local government input on jurisdictional, tax, and related issues like planning, and the NEPA process already requires analysis of land use issues, including potential impacts and mitigation of those impacts on local governments and services, and provides several opportunities for public hearing and comment. In addition, most proposed gaming-related trust land acquisitions already include agreements with local communities (or some other vehicle to address the concerns of local governments) in order to provide for the mitigation of impacts from proposed gaming projects. But as Ms. Dillon acknowledged in her testimony, some non-Indian communities/local governments will never consent to tribal land acquisition, regardless of the merits or purpose for the acquisition. To give those communities effective veto authority would be neither appropriate nor consistent with the purposes of the IRA.

During the hearing, it was suggested that local government participation in the process could be strengthened by including in a *Carcieri* fix some kind of requirement that a tribe enter into a "voluntary" memoranda of understanding ("MOU") with local communities affected by a proposed tribal land acquisition for off-reservation gaming. Apart from the fact that it is unclear how a statutory requirement could impose a voluntary agreement, this type of requirement is troubling because it could allow non-Indian communities to exact a high price from a newly recognized or restored tribe (which has limited options because of existing regulatory historical and modern connections requirements) in exchange for allowing a gaming acquisition to proceed, or to delay the process indefinitely, or to simply refuse to negotiate a all. While the Cowlitz Tribe fully supports voluntary agreements with local communities, and like most tribes desires to forge positive, productive, mutually beneficial relationships with its neighbors, we are concerned that this type of provision is not appropriate to include in a *Carcieri* fix and would effectively hand over the Federal Government's decision-making authority to local governments. Or, as in the case of Cowlitz, where our MOU with Clark County was challenged and set aside under state law, a hostile third-party effectively could derail the fee-to-trust process by challenging the MOU. We believe that the existing rules already provide local communities with ample opportunity to participate in and comment on the impacts of proposed tribal gaming acquisitions, and require the Department to address issues raised by local communities. The law should not be changed to give non-Indian communities or interested third parties veto power over where (or even whether) newly recognized or restored tribes may acquire land in trust for gaming.

The Cowlitz Tribe understands that enactment of clean *Carcieri*-fix legislation is a very significant challenge. Nevertheless, we add our voices to those of the Obama Administration, the National Congress of American Indians (NCAI), the United South and Eastern Tribes, and tribes throughout Indian Country in asking Congress to enact a fix that puts all federally recognized tribes on an equal playing field, and does so without imposing draconian new restrictions on fee-to-trust acquisitions. Chairwoman Cantwell and Vice Chairman Barrasso, and members of the Committee, we again appreciate your commitment to achieving an honorable *Carcieri* fix.

PREPARED STATEMENT OF HON. CRAIG CORN, CHAIRMAN, MENOMINEE INDIAN TRIBE

My name is Craig Corn, and I am the Chairman of the Menominee Indian Tribe of Wisconsin ("Menominee Tribe"). We are located in Menominee County, Wisconsin. I appreciate the opportunity to provide this statement for the record regarding the hearing held on the *Carcieri* issue.

The Menominee Tribe does not have a *Carcieri* issue, because it was a federally-recognized tribe in 1934. The Department of Interior ("DOI") can therefore acquire lands in trust for the Menominee under the Indian Reorganization Act notwithstanding *Carcieri*. We submit this statement for the record, however, to respond to Senator Feinstein's testimony provided at the hearing, in which she addressed off-reservation gaming acquisitions, and specifically testified in favor of enactment of S. 477, a bill she has sponsored which would establish new requirements for off-reservation trust acquisitions for gaming. I am submitting this statement because enactment of S. 477 could negatively impact the Menominee's application to acquire off-reservation trust land in Kenosha, Wisconsin, for gaming.

First, a bit of background. In 2004, Menominee submitted its application to acquire off-reservation trust lands in Kenosha for gaming purposes, and requesting that DOI make the "two-part" determination under the Indian Gaming Regulatory Act ("IGRA"). In August of this year, nine years later, DOI made a favorable two-part determination, finding that (1) the acquisition was in the best interest of the Menominee Tribe and, (2) that it was not detrimental to the surrounding community. Under the IGRA, the Governor of Wisconsin must now concur in the determination. If he concurs, then, under current law, DOI could acquire the lands in trust for Menominee and we could conduct gaming on the lands.

S. 477 would change existing law, however, to require DOI to make additional findings before the lands could be acquired for gaming. For our Tribe, imposition of new requirements, now would further delay a cumbersome process that has already taken nine years. They could also lead to litigation by opponents of tribal gaming.

Any new requirements in S. 477 are unnecessary. The current two-part determination process is very difficult to satisfy, and no further requirements are necessary. In the twenty-five years since enactment of IGRA, only 8 tribes have been authorized to conduct off-reservation gaming under the two-part determination procedure. The DOI does not rubber stamp off-reservation gaming acquisitions, as shown by its record in general, and the nine years it has taken us to obtain a two-part determination. Further, the two-part determination requires concurrence by the state governor, a truly unique requirement in federal law that fully protects state sovereignty.

The acquisition on behalf of the Menominee Tribe enjoys the overwhelming support of the local community as demonstrated by resolutions from the City and County where the lands are located, and favorable referenda by both the City and County as well. The project will create over 3,000 jobs and contribute significantly to the local economy. The Tribe entered into an intergovernmental agreement with the City and County to mitigate any possible impacts and to provide for services to the planned facility. DOI correctly determined that the proposed casino would not be detrimental to the surrounding community.

DOI also correctly determined that the proposed casino would be in the best interest of the Tribe and its members. The Menominee Tribe has over 8,860 members who rely upon the Tribe to provide necessary governmental services including healthcare, law enforcement, education, and post-secondary education. The Tribe has significant unmet needs due in large part to the lingering impacts of the Tribe's termination in the 1950s, and the gaming project will help the Tribe meet those needs. Menominee County (which is coterminous with the reservation and 90% of its population are tribal members) is the poorest county in Wisconsin, with the highest unemployment and worst health indicators.

In summary, S. 477 would unfairly impose new, unnecessary, and vague requirements on the Menominee nine years after it submitted its application and after it received a favorable two-part determination, and while the determination is before Wisconsin Governor Scott Walker. Even if the Committee were to consider S. 477 (or any other limitations on gaming on off-reservation lands), it should first hold a hearing on those proposed changes in order to provide the Committee with the views of all parties, tribal and non-tribal, that might be impacted by the proposed changes.

Thank you for the opportunity to share my views with the Committee.

———

PREPARED STATEMENT OF THE TOHONO O'ODHAM NATION

As Chairwoman Cantwell so eloquently said in her opening statement, the Supreme Court's 2009 decision in *Carcieri v. Salazar* has created two unequal classes of federally recognized tribes—tribes that are able to benefit from the Indian Reorganization Act (IRA) and tribes that are not. Since the IRA is in many ways the fundamental backbone of modern federal Indian law, this disparity has caused significant injustices. The Nation applauds the Committee's continuing effort to find a path forward to enact an honorable fix to the damage *Carcieri* has caused Indian Country.

While the Nation was not directly affected by the *Carcieri* decision—as its status as a tribe "under federal jurisdiction" in 1934 is beyond dispute—the Nation has consistently expressed its unequivocal support for federal legislation that would undo the very real damage that *Carcieri* has wreaked on so many federally recognized tribes. As one of the largest tribes in the United States, the Nation feels an obligation to speak out in support of tribes that have been less fortunate—tribes that were terminated, tribes that were or are landless, and tribes that, for other reasons, have suffered the devastating effects of having an inadequate homeland. The Nation well understands these deprivations, as nearly 10,000 acres of the Nation's own reservation land were taken by the United States in the mid-twentieth century, and the tribal members residing on those lands were forced to crowd together on a small 40-acre parcel of land. We know what it is like to lose our traditional land, and we know how hard it is to try to acquire replacement land. For some tribes, the *Carcieri* decision has made acquiring new land impossible.

The Nation understands that the Committee may eventually consider specific legislative language, and the Nation likely will submit more specific comments after that proposed language becomes available. In the meantime, the Nation would like to bring to the Committee's attention significant misstatements in written testimony submitted by a witness at the November 20, 2013, hearing that were directed at the Nation. In addition, the Nation feels compelled to express its concerns about several suggested new limitations on taking land in trust that were discussed by some witnesses at the November 20, 2013 hearing. The Nation will address each of these matters in turn.

A. The Nation's Proposed West Valley Resort

In her written testimony, Senator Dianne Feinstein made the following statement:

> The City of Glendale, Arizona, is disputing the Tohono O'odham (Toe-hoe-no OH-tham) Nation's proposal to open a casino and resort in the city's urban sport and entertainment district, which even by the tribe's own admission is at least 75 miles from its reservation's border.

Testimony of Senator Diane Feinstein, at 4.

This statement, which was directed at the Tohono O'odham Nation's replacement lands acquisition for its West Valley Resort project near the cities of Glendale and Peoria in Maricopa County, Arizona, is incorrect in several key respects. First, the West Valley Resort enjoys widespread support from nearby communities. In fact, three neighboring communities, Peoria, Tolleson, and Surprise, have passed resolutions in support of the Nation's project. What is more, as has been widely reported, the City of Glendale has begun a productive dialogue with the Nation.[1] Second, contrary to Senator Feinstein's statement, the Resort site is not "at least 75 miles from [the Nation's] borders." In fact, as the Nation has repeatedly testified, the West Valley Resort property is only about 48 miles from the Nation's existing trust land at San Lucy Village, near Gila Bend, Arizona (where its land was flooded and destroyed) and is located in the same county (Maricopa) as this existing trust land.[2]

B. Other Limitations on the Fee-to-Trust Process Discussed at the Hearing

1. The Proposed "Aboriginal Ties" Requirement Will Lead to Unjust and Perverse Results

As a consequence of the Removal Era, culminating in the Indian Removal Act of 1830, many tribes ceded their aboriginal territories in the Eastern United States and were forcibly removed to areas west of the Mississippi River. Act of May 28, 1830, ch. 148, Stat. 411. Many of the tribal victims of the removal era were widely dispersed, and some have only recently achieved federal acknowledgment and/or obtained reservations. Similar displacement occurred in the Western United States as well, such that not all tribes today reside in their aboriginal territories. To graft an across-the-board aboriginal ties requirement onto the IRA's trust land acquisition authority would impose a great injustice for some tribes, and lead to absurd results for others, because in the modern era some tribes simply are not currently located within the confines of their aboriginal territories. Indeed, some tribes' aboriginal territories are not even located within the same states or the same regions of the country as where the tribes currently are located.[3]

Depending on how it might be formulated, an aboriginal ties requirement also could have an unintentional adverse impact on the Nation. In the Nation's land claim settlement, Congress explicitly identified the three counties within which the Nation would be entitled to acquire new land to replace lands destroyed by the Army Corps of Engineers (*i.e.*, the same three counties in which the Nation already has other reservation lands). Imposition of an aboriginal ties requirement on the Nation's land claim settlement could significantly and inappropriately alter the settlement terms agreed to by the Nation and the United States nearly three decades ago.

---

[1] Carolyn Dryer, Ed., *Dialogue has begun; partnership appears on horizon*, Glendale Star, September 15, 2013 (available at *http://www.glendalestar.com/opinion/editorials/arti- cle\4408fed6-11a6-11e3-9130-001a4bcf887a.html*)

[2] Although not pertinent under the Nation's land settlement, the West Valley Resort property is a readily commutable distance from Gila Bend. Indeed, "almost twice as many workers leave the Gila Bend area to commute to jobs in the East Valley as stay to work in Gila Bend. East Valley consists of Scottsdale, Paradise Valley, Fountain Hills, Tempe, Mesa, Gilbert and Chandler." *Creating New Avenues for Success: The West Valley Workforce and Labor Market Study*, 2008, pp. 53–54 (sponsored by WESTMARC, a coalition of fifteen West Valley communities). The East Valley cities to which the majority of Gila Bend's workers commute are significantly farther from Gila Bend than is the West Valley Resort property.

[3] The reality is that, when Indian gaming comes into play, the Department of the Interior's own regulations generally already require the Secretary to consider a tribe's *historical* (as opposed to *aboriginal*) connections to the land at issue before she will decide whether to acquire land for gaming for newly recognized or newly restored tribes. The only instances in which historical ties are not required are when lands are acquired as part of a "two-part determination" (in which cases the Governor of the State has absolute veto authority) and when lands are acquired in the settlement of a land claim (in which cases the Department follows Congress' specific direction, since land claim settlements generally are implemented through acts of Congress).

2. Requiring MOUs with Local Counties Also May Lead to Unjust Results

Another potential restriction on the fee-to-trust process discussed at the hearing would require tribes and neighboring non-Indian communities to enter into memoranda of understanding (MOUs) before the Secretary could acquire land in trust for tribes. Like many tribes, the Nation has always worked closely with its neighboring communities to deal with the kinds of issues that all governments regularly address, including water and power, transportation, and public safety, and we are proud of the many mutually beneficial agreements that we share with local non-Indian communities.

For these issues to be addressed in a fair, equitable, and mutually agreeable manner, however, the Nation believes that discussions must take place in an environment of mutual respect and trust, not one of coercion. Further, the Nation is aware that, in some circumstances, a tribe may have very little latitude on where it can acquire lands. In our case, our Federal land claim settlement requires that we acquire our replacement land in one of three counties. If an MOU requirement was grafted onto our land claim settlement, then local governments could unilaterally block implementation of our Federal land claim settlement, if they were of a mind to do so, completely undermining the long-recognized Federal trust obligation owed to the Nation as an Indian tribe.

Accordingly, the Nation opposes a condition on the IRA that would unfairly interfere in intergovernmental discussions and the Federal trust obligation by requiring that a tribe enter into agreements with surrounding communities *before* the acquisition of lands in trust for a tribe.

Finally, the Nation urges the Committee to consider grandfathering existing fee-to-trust decisions that have not yet been fully implemented to protect tribes, like the Nation, that have spent many years and expended significant resources to navigate the existing process. Failure to include such a grandfathering provision will effectively punish tribes that have been playing by the rules in good faith.

Conclusion

The Nation supports the Committee's efforts to ensure that the IRA applies to all tribes. However, the concerns raised by some witnesses relate only to gaming issues and do not belong in legislation designed to address the injustices of the *Carcieri* decision. The Nation urges that some of the trust acquisition restrictions suggested by some witnesses are inconsistent with the primary purposes of the Reorganization Act and, if adopted, may result in unforeseen and unjust consequences.

We hope these comments are helpful to the Committee, and the Nation is happy to answer any questions the Committee might have.

————

PREPARED STATEMENT OF MATTHEW D. CHASE, EXECUTIVE DIRECTOR, NATIONAL ASSOCIATION OF COUNTIES (NACO)

Dear Chairwoman Cantwell and Vice Chairman Barrasso:

On behalf of the nation's 3,069 counties, we thank you for the opportunity to submit the following statement to the Senate Committee on Indian Affairs as you consider such a critical issue for county and tribal governments. We submit for the Committee's consideration our statement that provides the National Association of Counties' (NACo) relevant policy, determined and approved by our full membership, as it pertains to county and tribal government relationships and to the Supreme Court decision in *Carcieri v. Salazar*, 555 U.S. 379 (2009).

NACo is the only national organization that represents county governments in the United States. Founded in 1935, NACo advances issues with a unified voice before the Federal Government, improves the public's understanding of county government, assists counties in finding and sharing innovative solutions through education and research and provides value-added services to save counties and taxpayers money. As part of its work, NACo is engaged in pursuing federal laws and regulations that provide the framework for constructive government-to-government relationships between counties and tribes.

County and Tribal Government Relations

The policy of NACo is to support government-to-government relations that recognize the role and unique interests of tribes, states, counties and other local governments to protect all members of their communities and to provide governmental services and infrastructure beneficial to all—Indian and non-Indian alike.

NACo recognizes and respects the tribal right of self-governance to provide for tribal members and to preserve traditional tribal culture and heritage. In similar fashion, NACo recognizes and promotes self-governance by counties to provide for the health, safety and general welfare of all members of their communities. To that end, NACo supports active participation by counties on issues and activities that have an impact on counties.

NACo supports tribes and local governments reaching enforceable agreements concerning the mitigation of impacts of gaming or other development. NACo opposes any federal limitation on the ability of tribes, states, counties and other local governments to reach mutually acceptable and enforceable agreements or on the ability of these governments to fulfill the purposes for which they have self-governance.

Nothing in federal law should interfere with the provision of public health, safety, welfare, or environmental services by local government. It is the policy of NACo to support legislation and regulation that preserves—and does not impair—the ability of counties to provide these services to the community.

Lands in Trust

NACo supports the improvement of the process by which lands are considered to be taken into trust, such as revising the Indian Reorganization Act of 1934 (IRA) to require adequate advance notice of applications, actual meaningful consultation (including providing counties 120 days to respond to applications and requiring the Department of the Interior/Bureau of Indian Affairs to respond within 90 days, in writing, to such comments explaining the rationale for acceptance or rejection of those comments) and (to the extent constitutionally permissible) the consent of the affected counties.

NACo opposes administrative action or a legislative "quick fix" to overturn the United States Supreme Court decision in the case of *Carcieri v. Salazar*, which held that the Secretary of the U.S. Department of the Interior (DOI) lacks authority to take land into trust for tribes that were not "under federal jurisdiction" upon enactment of the IRA in 1934. NACo calls on Congress to address any *Carcieri* issues as part of a comprehensive examination and reform of the fee land into trust process.

This reform is necessary as the current federal fee to trust process, as exercised under the IRA and as used under the "restored lands" exception to the Indian Gaming Regulatory Act (IGRA), is contrary to the original legislative intent; is without clear and enforceable standards; does not take into account county interests; and, at times, interferes with county ability to provide essential services to the community. NACo supports legislative changes to the trust process that also include full compensation to counties for lost tax revenue resulting from taking lands into federal jurisdiction.

Once again, thank you for the opportunity to comment and provide NACo's policy.

JOINT PREPARED STATEMENT OF TRIBAL ORGANIZATIONS

Dear Chairwoman Cantwell, Vice Chairman Barrasso, Chairman Hastings, Ranking Member DeFazio, Chairman Young, and Ranking Member Hanabusa:

Our undersigned Tribal organizations have come together to make this joint petition to the Senate Indian Affairs Committee and the House Natural Resources Committee and Subcommittee on Indian and Alaska Native Affairs urging that you work with us to ensure swift enactment of legislation to address the Supreme Court's misguided decision in *Carcieri v. Salazar*, 555 U.S. 379 (2009). Indian Tribes across the country are suffering significant direct negative economic, community, and cultural impacts from this decision and these impacts are increasing exponentially with each day that the Court's decision is not addressed by Congress.

We thank Rep. Tom Cole, now Senator Ed Markey, and Rep. Colleen Hanabusa for introducing H.R. 279 and H.R. 666, respectively, in the 113th Congress to remedy this situation. These bills enjoy bi-partisan support. Further, these proposals are not only budget neutral but also will save the federal government money that is currently being expended to defend itself from mushrooming litigation. The House passed *Carcieri* language as part of the year-long Fiscal Year 2011 Continuing Resolution, which the Senate unfortunately did not pass.

Congress enacted the Indian Reorganization Act (IRA) in 1934 in response to devastating federal policies that resulted in a loss of millions of acres of Tribal lands. An overarching goal of the IRA was to restore and protect Tribal homelands so that Tribes would prosper both politically and economically. Up to the time of the *Carcieri* decision, the Department of the Interior consistently construed the IRA to authorize the Secretary of Interior to place land into trust for any Tribe so long as that Tribe was federally recognized at the time of the trust application. We simply seek legislation that restores the *status quo ante*.

The ability of Tribes, working with the Secretary, to have land taken into trust is central to both Tribal sovereignty and the Federal trust responsibility. Moreover, it is the foundation of Tribal efforts to strengthen our self-determination and to ensure that we protect our cultural identities. Pursuant to the IRA and in furtherance of the Federal government's policy of Tribal self-determination, DOI for over 75 years has assisted Tribal governments in placing land into trust, enabling Tribes to rebuild their homelands to provide essential governmental services through the construction of schools, health clinics, hospitals, Head Start centers, elder centers, veterans centers, housing, and community centers. The IRA's trust acquisition provisions have also assisted Tribes in protecting their traditions, cultures, and customs. Tribal trust acquisitions also play a significant role in Tribal economic development, as well as job and wealth creation in Tribal communities and surrounding non-Indian communities.

In *Carcieri*, the Supreme Court construed the IRA to limit the Secretary's authority to place land into trust to only those Tribes that were "under federal jurisdiction" as of 1934. This ruling jeopardizes the ability for all federally recognized Tribes to rebuild their communities and provide critical programs. The legal ambiguities resulting from *Carcieri* have further delayed the already severely backlogged land-into-trust process. The decision also raises significant safety concerns, as it opens the door to challenging criminal convictions for crimes that occurred on Indian land. Further, *Carcieri* has generated -- and will continue to generate if unaddressed -- considerable legal disputes over proposed and existing trust acquisitions in which the United States, at taxpayer expense, is a defendant.

We thank you for your efforts thus far on this matter and look forward to continuing our work together on passage of this critical legislation.

Sincerely,

Jefferson Keel, President
National Congress of American Indians

Brian Patterson, President
United South and Eastern Tribes

Kevin J. Allis, Executive Director
Native American Contractors Association

Mark Romero, Chairman
CATG Board of Directors

Fawn Sharp, President
Affiliated Tribes of Northwest Indians

Cathy Abramson, Chairwoman
National Indian Health Board

Cheryl A. Causley, Chairperson
Native American Indian Housing Council

Dr. Heather Shotton, President
National Indian Education Association

W. Ron Allen, Chairman
Self-Governance Communication & Education Tribal Consortium

Terry Rambler, President
Inter Tribal Council of Arizona

Jacki Haight, President
National Indian Head Start Directors Association

Bill Lomax, President
Native American Finance Officers Association

Gary Davis, President
National Center for American Indian Enterprise Development, NCAIED

Ryan Wilson, President
National Alliance to Save Native Languages

Michele Stanley, President
Midwest Alliance of Sovereign Tribes

LaDonna Harris, President
Americans for Indian Opportunity

Michael E. Roberts, President
First Nations Development Institute

Ben Shelly, President
Navajo Nation

Julie Kitka, President
Alaska Federation of Natives

Melbert "Moke" Eaglefeathers, President
National Council of Urban Indian Health

Lynn Valbuena, Chairwoman
Tribal Alliance of Sovereign Indian Nations

Harlan Beaulieu, President
Intertribal Agriculture Council

Tex Hall
Co-Chairman, COLT
Chairman, Great Plains Tribal Chairman Association

John E. Echohawk, Executive Director
Native American Rights Fund

Robert "Tim" Coulter, Executive Director
Indian Law Resource Center

Cris Stainbrook, President
Indian Land Tenure Foundation

Robert Smith, Chairman of the Board
Southern California Tribal Chairmen's Association

Ernie Stevens, Jr., Chairman
National Indian Gaming Association

Tribal Leaders
Urge the United States Congress
to Enact *Carcieri* Fix Legislation

Dear Senator/Representative:

On behalf of the Native Nations, organizations and communities that we represent, we write to respectfully urge you to work to enact legislation to rectify the significant damage to Indian Country that has been caused by the Supreme Court's 2009 decision in *Carcieri v. Salazar*, 555 U.S. 379 (2009). That misguided decision inadvertently has created substantial inequities, creating an arbitrary divide by which some federally recognized tribes may no longer be eligible for the very same essential benefits available to all other federally recognized tribes under the Indian Reorganization Act of 1934 (IRA). Only Congress can rectify this modern-day injustice -- only Congress can ensure that all federally recognized tribes will be treated equally under the law.

More specifically, it is critical that the U.S. Congress enact a *Carcieri* fix to clarify the Secretary of the Interior's authority to acquire land in trust for *all* federally recognized tribes. The ability of tribes, working with the Secretary consistent with well-established federal regulations, to acquire adequate land is essential to our ability to provide essential governmental services to our people through the construction of schools, health clinics, hospitals, Head Start centers, elder centers, veterans centers, housing, and community centers. The IRA's trust acquisition provisions are essential to these efforts. Tribal trust acquisitions also play a significant role in tribal economic development as well as job creation in tribal communities and surrounding non-Indian communities.

During the seventy-five years before the *Carcieri* decision was handed down, the Department of the Interior consistently (and we think correctly) construed the 1934 Indian Reorganization Act (IRA) to authorize the Secretary of the Interior to place land into trust for all tribes so long as that tribe was federally recognized at the time of the trust application. In *Carcieri*, the Supreme Court changed that by construing the IRA to limit the Secretary's authority to place land into trust only for those tribes that were "under federal jurisdiction" as of 1934. This ruling jeopardizes the ability of all federally recognized tribes to rebuild their communities and provide critical programs. The legal ambiguities resulting from *Carcieri* have further delayed the already severely backlogged land-into-trust process. Also, due to *Carcieri*, tribes are finding it increasingly difficult to secure financing for economic development projects that would create jobs in these tough times given questions raised about the status of lands on which these projects would be located. The decision also raises significant safety concerns, as it opens the door to challenging criminal convictions for crimes that occurred on Indian land. Further, *Carcieri* has generated -- and will continue to generate if unaddressed -- considerable legal disputes over proposed and existing trust acquisitions in which the United States, at taxpayer expense, is a defendant.

In sum, a simple *Carcieri* fix which makes clear that the Secretary of the Interior should resume treating federally recognized tribes equally in her implementation of the Indian Reorganization Act is all that we ask for. Such a fix would be budget neutral. More importantly, it would be a great and admirable milestone in the United States' history of its relationship with Indian tribes, a signal that the United States' relationship with tribal governments in the twenty-first century will be characterized by fair and honorable dealings.

We thank you for your consideration of our request, and we look forward to continuing to work with you on passage of this critical legislation.

Sincerely,

Name	Native Nation/Org./Community	Name	Native Nation/Org./Community
W. Ron Allen	Chairman, Jamestown S'Klallam		Tribal Council, Quinault Indian Nation
	Native Village of Eklutna		Absentee Shawnee Tribe of Indians of Oklahoma
	Central Council Tlingit Haida Indian Tribes of Alaska		Principal Chief, Sac and Fox Nation

65

Name	Native Nation/Org/Community
(signature)	Nome Eskimo Community
(signature)	Chief, Mohegan Tribe of Indians of Connecticut; Chairperson Tribal Self-Governance Advisory Committee for IHS
(signature)	Chairman, Alabama Coushatta Tribe of Texas
(signature)	Vice-Chairwoman, Alabama Coushatta Tribe of Texas
(signature)	Chief, Aroostook Band of Micmacs
(signature)	Chief, Catawba Indian Nation
(signature)	Vice-Chief, Catawba Indian Nation
(signature)	Chitimacha Tribe of Louisiana
(signature)	Vice-Chairwoman, Coushatta Tribe of Louisiana
(signature)	Council Member, Coushatta Tribe of Louisiana

Name	Native Nation/Org/Community
(signature)	Vice-Chief, Passamaquoddy Tribe – Indian Township
(signature)	Councilman, Passamaquoddy Tribe – Indian Township
(signature)	Nation Liaison, Oneida Nation
(signature)	Chairman, Tunica-Biloxi Tribe of Louisiana
(signature)	MOWA Band of Choctaw Indians
(signature)	Nanticoke Conoi-Canoe
(signature)	Nanticoke of Delaware
(signature)	Organized Village of Saxman
(signature)	Lac Vieux Desert
(signature)	Councilman, Alabama Coushatta Tribe of Texas
(signature)	Native Village of Tanana, AK

Name	Native Nation/Org/Community
(signature)	Principal Chief Michell Hicks, Eastern Band of Cherokee Indians
(signature)	Chief, Houlton Band of Maliseet Indians
(signature)	Tribal Council, Houlton Band of Maliseet Indians
(signature)	Chief, Jena Band of Choctaw Indians, LA
(signature)	Councilman, Jena Band of Choctaw Indians, LA
(signature)	Chairman, Mashantucket Pequot Tribal Nation
(signature)	Chief, Mississippi Band of Choctaw Indians
(signature)	Vice-Chief, Mississippi Band of Choctaw Indians
(signature)	Council, Tunica-Biloxi Tribe of Louisiana
(signature)	Councilman, Narragansett Tribe
(signature)	Vice-Chairman, Mohegan Tribe of Connecticut

Name	Native Nation/Org/Community
(signature)	Native Village of Tanana, AK
(signature)	Native Village of Tanana, AK
(signature)	Tanana Tribal Council
(signature)	Sault Ste. Marie Tribe of Chippewa
(signature)	Big Pine Paiute Tribe of California
(signature)	Kialegee Tribal Town
(signature)	Pueblo of Acoma Tribal Council
(signature)	Central Council
(signature)	Shawnee Tribe
(signature)	Native Village of Tanacross
(signature)	Santo Domingo Pueblo

Name	Native Nation/Org./Community	Name	Native Nation/Org./Community
(signature)	Pawnee Nation of Oklahoma	*(signature)*	Ohkay Owingeh, New Mexico
(signature)	Saginaw Chippewa	*(signature)*	Ohkay Owingeh, New Mexico
(signature)	Cherokee Nation	*(signature)*	Ohkay Owingeh, New Mexico
(signature)	Iowa Tribe of Oklahoma	*(signature)*	Ohkay Owingeh, New Mexico
(signature)	Native Village of Venetie	*(signature)*	Ohkay Owingeh, New Mexico
(signature)	Klamath Tribes	*(signature)*	Ohkay Owingeh, New Mexico
(signature)	Fallon Paiute-Shoshone Tribe	*(signature)*	Pueblo of Laguna
(signature)	Nez Perce Tribe	*(signature)*	Pueblo of Laguna
(signature)	Vice-Chairwoman, Mashpee Wampanoag Tribe	*(signature)*	Ohkay Owingeh, New Mexico
(signature)	Cherokee	*(signature)*	Mohegan Tribe
(signature)	Ohkay Owingeh, New Mexico	*(signature)*	Lumbee Tribe of North Carolina

Name	Native Nation/Org./Community
(signature)	Councilman, Narragansett Tribe
(signature)	Timbisha Shoshone
(signature)	Fort Independence Paiute Tribe
(signature)	United Keetoowah Band of Cherokee
(signature)	Cherokee Nation
(signature)	Picuris Pueblo
(signature)	Muscogee Creek
(signature)	Tlingit & Haida
(signature)	Cheyenne River
(signature)	Chippewa Cree
(signature)	Mashpee Wampanoag Tribe

Name	Native Nation/Org./Community	Name	Native Nation/Org./Community
[signature]	Native Village of Ambler	*[signature]*	Sisseton Wahpeton Oyate
[signature]	Chief, Haliwa-Saponi Indian Tribe	*[signature]*	Chairwoman, Eastern Band of Cherokee Indians
[signature]	Chief, Muscogee Creek Nation	*[signature]*	Tule River Tribe of California
[signature]	Osage Nation	*[signature]*	Cherokee Nation
[signature]	Osage Nation	*[signature]*	Cherokee Nation
[signature]	Spokane Tribe	*[signature]*	Cherokee Nation
[signature]	Scotts Valley Pomo	*[signature]*	Cherokee Nation
[signature]	Tuolumne Band of Mewuk Indians	*[signature] Jon Overcash*	Cherokee Nation
[signature]	Native Village of Tanana	*Brad Perry*	Cherokee Nation
[signature]	Hualapai Tribe of Arizona	*[signature]*	Cherokee Nation
[signature]	Soboba Band of Luiseno Indians	*[signature]*	Cherokee Nation
[signature]	Cherokee Nation	*[signature]*	Tohono O'odham Nation
[signature]	Cherokee Nation	*[signature]*	Tohono O'odham Nation
Scott Bighorse	Assistant Chief, Osage Nation	*[signature]*	Tohono O'odham Nation
Georgiana Hotch	Chilkoot Indian Association	*[signature]*	Tohono O'odham Nation
Harriet Brouillette	Chilkoot Indian Association	*[signature]*	Tohono O'odham Nation
Theodore Hart	Chilkoot Indian Association	*[signature]*	Tohono O'odham Nation
[signature]	Chilkoot Indian Association	*[signature]*	Tohono O'odham Nation
Stephen G. Smith	Kiowa Business Committee	*[signature]*	Cowlitz Tribe
Marie B. Kuahara	General Council, Vice-Chair Yakama Nation	*[signature]*	Poarch Band of Creek Indians, AL
[signature]	Assistant Chief, Seminole Nation	*[signature]*	Native Village of Afognak, AK
[signature]	Principal Chief, Seminole Nation of OK	*[signature]*	Native Village of Buckland, AK

Name	Native Nation/Org./Community	Name	Native Nation/Org./Community
(signature)	President, Pawnee Nation	*(signature)*	Chairman, Mashpee Wampanoag
(signature)	Pawnee Nation Council	*(signature)*	Bishop Paiute Tribal Council
(signature)	Vice President, Pawnee Nation	*(signature)*	Choctaw Apache Community of Ebarb, LA
(signature)	First Lt. Governor Pueblo of Laguna	*(signature)*	Treasurer, Squaxin Island
Kim Barber	Navajo Nation	*(signature)* Quan Meleng	Reno-Sparks Indian Colony
Virginia Hill	Iipay Nation of Santa Ysabel	*(signature)*	Muscogee Creek
(signature)	Quinault Nation NA	Lucinda Cruchiun	Muscogee Creek
(signature)	Shoalwater Bay Tribe	*(signature)*	Berry Creek Rancheria of Maidu Indians of California
(signature)	Lummi Nation	*(signature)*	Tribal Council, Berry Creek Rancheria of Maidu Indians of California
(signature)	Seneca Nation of Indians	Sharlene Bernett	Muscogee Nation
(signature)	Native Village of Eagle	*(signature)*	Cherokee Nation
Troy Elliott	Chickasaw Nation	Mary Lou Mills	Kanakos Indian Tribe
(signature)	Muscogee Creek	*(signature)*	Crow Tribe
(signature)	Tribal Council, Tohono O'odham Nation	*(signature)*	Lac Vieux Desert
Kiona Zaun	Cortina Rancheria	*(signature)*	Rincon Band of Luiseno
(signature)	Mo-Chis Lower Creek	Flavio Pacheco	Santo Domingo Pueblo, New Mexico
(signature)	Eastern Band of Cherokee Indians	Susu Mahogami	Havasuville Indian Community
(signature)	Muscogee Creek	*(signature)*	Echota Tribe of Alabama
(signature)	Muscogee Creek	*(signature)*	Oto-Missouria Tribe
(signature)	Sisseton Wahpeton Oyate	*(signature)*	Round Valley BIA, ED
(signature)	Muscogee Creek	Paul Peters	Round Valley Indian House
(signature)	Round Valley Indian Tribes	*(signature)*	Lhac, Agua Caliente
		(signature)	Chalkyitsik

Name	Native Nation/Org./Community	Name	Native Nation/Org./Community
	President, Pawnee Nation		Chairman, Mashpee Wampanoag
	Pawnee Nation Council		Bishop Paiute Tribal Council
	Vice President, Pawnee Nation		Choctaw Apache Community of Ebach, LA
	First Lt. Governor Pueblo of Laguna		Treasurer, Squaxin Island
	Navajo Nation		Reno-Sparks Indian Colony
	Ipay Nation of Santa Ysabel		Muscogee Creek
	Quinault Nation NA		Muscogee Creek
	Shoalwater Bay Tribe		Berry Creek Rancheria of Maidu Indians of California
	Lummi Nation		Tribal Council, Berry Creek Rancheria of Maidu Indians of California
	Seneca Nation of Indians		Muscogee Nation
	Native Village of Eagle		Cherokee Nation
	Chickasaw Nation		Kanaksu Indian Tribe
	Muscogee Creek		Crow Tribe
	Tribal Council, Tohono O'odham Nation		Los Vieux Desert
	Cortina Rancheria		Rincon Band of Luiseno
	Mo-Chis Lower Creek		Santo Domingo Pueblo, New Mexico
	Eastern Band of Cherokee Indians		Heuschville Indian Community
	Muscogee Creek		Echota Tribe of Alabama
	Muscogee Creek		Oto-Missouria Tribe
	Sisseton Wahpeton Oyate		Round Valley IHA, ED
	Muscogee Creek		Round Valley Indian Homes
	Round Valley Indian Tribes		Chac, Agua Caliente
			Chalkyitsik

RESPONSE TO WRITTEN QUESTIONS SUBMITTED BY HON. MARIA CANTWELL TO DIANE DILLON

Question 1. Has CSAC taken a position on tribal sovereignty?

Answer. CSAC's adopted policy affirms the association's recognition and respect for tribal self-governance to provide for its members and to preserve traditional Indian culture and heritage. CSAC's policy also states support for cooperative and respectful government-to-government relations that recognize the interdependent role of tribes, counties, and other local governments to be responsive to the needs and concerns of all members of their respective communities.

As reiterated in past and recent congressional testimony, CSAC has great respect for the authority granted to all federally recognized Indian tribes. It is CSAC's intent to pursue policies that respect tribal authority, while at the same time protecting counties' legitimate interests, including the legal responsibility to provide for the health, safety, environment, infrastructure, and general welfare of all citizens.

Question 2. Did counties have issues with the fee-to-trust process or take a formal position on the process prior to passage of the Indian Gaming Regulatory Act (IGRA)?

Answer. Although CSAC did not have a formal position on the BIA's fee-to-trust process prior to the 1988 enactment of IGRA, many individual California counties were experiencing impacts in rural areas from Indian gaming establishments. These early establishments were places where Indian bingo was the primary commercial enterprise in support of tribal economic self-reliance. The impacts on local communities were not as significant in large part because the facilities where Indian bingo was played were modest in size and did not attract as many patrons as larger casinos that have proliferated today. Following the enactment of IGRA, the impacts to counties from Indian gaming enterprises increased with the advent of larger facilities. Even so, the impacts to local communities from these larger facilities were generally manageable, except in certain instances.

Beginning with the 1999 signing of the State's Tribal Gaming Compacts, the ensuing rapid expansion of Indian gaming in California has had profound impacts beyond the boundaries of tribal lands. The majority California's counties now have a casino, a tribe petitioning for federal recognition, or are the site of a proposed casino plan. As the Committee is aware, many casino proposals relate to projects on land far from a tribe's ancestral territory.

In response to the rise of significant off-reservation impacts resulting from tribal gaming establishments, CSAC adopted formal policy on Indian gaming in 2003. The association adopted subsequent policy revisions and updates in order to emphasize the need for counties and tribal governments to each carry out their governmental responsibilities in a manner that respects the governmental responsibilities of the other.

Today, California has 111 federally recognized tribes, 59 of which operate 60 casinos. Moreover, there are currently 352 applications for federal recognition pending nationwide, with one quarter of those from the state of California. With a large number of tribes already engaged in gaming and with the possibility that a significant number of additional tribal groups could gain federal recognition, CSAC and California's counties continue to take an active interest in federal Indian affairs issues and policies.

Question 3. Do California's counties have issues with the fee-to-trust process that aren't related to gaming?

Answer. Yes, California's counties have a number of concerns with the fee-to-trust process that are not related to tribal gaming. These concerns have become increasingly pressing, as California tribes have petitioned to have at least 9,938 acres of additional land taken into trust status for a variety of purposes since 2011 alone. As outlined in CSAC's congressional testimony, the association's fundamental concerns stem from the fact that there is a lack of clear and enforceable standards in the land-into-trust process. Congress has not set standards under which any delegated trust land authority would be applied by BIA. The relevant section of federal law, Section 5 of the *Indian Reorganization Act*, reads as follows: ''The Secretary of the Interior is hereby authorized in his discretion, to acquire [by various means] any interest in lands, water rights, or surface rights to lands, within or without reservations . . . for the purpose of providing land to Indians.'' 25 U.S.C. § 465.

The aforementioned general and undefined congressional guidance, as implemented by the Department of the Interior in its Part 151 regulations, has resulted in a trust land process that fails to meaningfully include the legitimate interests of local government agencies. Therefore, the concerns of California's counties are given minimal consideration in the fee-to-trust process, despite the fact that counties must address the off-reservation impacts of projects on trust lands and any inconsistencies with surrounding land uses, as well as provide some local government services, including law enforcement in California, on trust lands.

The lack of guidance has also led to procedural shortcomings in the fee-to-trust process. Local governments often do not receive timely notice when a trust land application is filed within their jurisdictions. In turn, BIA only invites comments from the affected state and the local governments with legal jurisdiction over the land

and, from those parties, only on the narrow question of tax revenue loss and regulatory jurisdictional conflicts. As a result, trust acquisition requests are reviewed under a very one-sided and incomplete record that does not provide real consultation or an adequate representation of the consequences of the decision. Moreover, local governments are often forced to resort to Freedom of Information Act requests to ascertain if petitions for Indian land determinations have been filed in their jurisdictions.

While CSAC remains particularly concerned that tribal gaming often leads to significant unmitigated impacts to the surrounding community, including environmental and economic impacts, other forms of tribal development also are a source of concern. For example, many tribal projects are often incompatible with local land-use plans and regulations (i.e. proposed tribal housing and associated infrastructure in areas that are zoned exclusively for agriculture). Moreover, economic development projects on trust lands that support existing Tribal gaming enterprises, for instance a golf course or music venue, can have off-reservation impacts similar to those of casinos. Unlike casino projects, which require negotiation of mitigation agreements with affected local governments under California's recent tribal-state gaming compacts, local governments have no ability to secure mitigation for the off-reservation impacts a project on trust lands may have on government services or the environment.

It should also be noted that many non-gaming trust acquisitions, both large and small, can result in jurisdictional confusion with regard to law enforcement, social service delivery, and emergency services. In addition, the loss of local control to regulate land uses without appropriate mitigation can congest county and state roadways, impact water quality in waterways, reduce water supply to adjacent properties, degrade habitat, air quality and the environment, and create a public nuisance. These types of impacts are not simply limited to the development and operation of Indian casinos.

Question 4. Have any California counties objected or sent remarks or testimony to the Department of the Interior (DOI) on a trust land application that was not related to gaming?

Answer. Yes, a number of California counties have sent comment letters to DOI/BIA regarding proposed non-gaming trust land acquisitions. For example, Fresno County sent a letter to BIA in 2012 regarding the Table Mountain Rancheria's application to have nine parcels of land taken into trust for non-gaming purposes. The County provided comments to the BIA in an effort to highlight a number of pertinent issues, including the expected loss of county property tax revenue and the continued provision of county services to the land.

Yolo County submitted comments in response to the Environmental Assessment and subsequent Finding of No Significant Impacts for the proposed acquisition of approximately 853 acres of land for the Yocha Dehe Wintun Nation in 2011 and 2013, respectively. The County raised no objections to the Tribe's proposed development of approximately 100 acres of the intended trust lands for housing, community facilities, infrastructure and cultural facilities. The Board of Supervisors was, however, concerned that there would be no mechanism for the County to provide meaningful input or secure mitigation measures for the off-reservation impacts of any future projects on the remaining 753 acres, for which no planned development was described in the Tribe's application.

Santa Barbara County recently sent correspondence to the BIA to register opposition to the Santa Ynez Band of Chumash Mission Indians' non-gaming fee-to-trust application. The parcel of land in question, which encompasses more than 1,400 acres, would be used for tribal housing and perhaps other non-gaming purposes, such as a major community center and an office complex. The County opposes the fee-to-trust application on the grounds that the proposed project conflicts with the County's General Plan, the Santa Ynez Community Plan, and local land-use regulations.

Additionally, if the land is taken into trust, Santa Barbara County would lose substantial tax revenue while at the same time experiencing an increased demand for services and infrastructure. In its correspondence to the BIA, the County notes that it is anticipated that the tribe may choose to change its intended uses on the site. Once the land is in trust, however, the County would have no regulatory authority in the approval process.

On a related matter, CSAC would like to highlight the fact that there are a number of tribes both within and outside the state of California that have switched the stated or intended uses of trust land. According to BIA records, land was taken into trust for the Smith River Rancheria in Del Norte County for tribal housing in 1989, only to be converted to gaming use in 1996.[1] In Butte County, a parcel of land was taken into trust for HUD tribal housing units and community uses in 1994; the land was converted to gaming in 1996.[2] Incidentally, in both of the aforementioned cases, National Indian Gaming Commission officials were not aware of applicable IGRA exceptions or status.

Thank you again for your leadership on this issue and for your consideration of our views.

––––––––

RESPONSE TO WRITTEN QUESTIONS SUBMITTED BY HON. JOHN BARRASSO TO DIANE DILLON

Question 1. What recommendations do you have for incentivizing local governments to enter into mitigation agreements?

Answer. CSAC believes that a strong incentive already exists for local governments, as well as tribes, to reach judicially enforceable agreements. For starters, the process of negotiating an agreement or memorandum-of-understanding (MOU) brings both parties to the table and often lays the foundation for a more productive, beneficial, and long-term government-to-government relationship. Moreover, a mitigation agreement provides the jurisdictional local government with certainty that the impacts of a particular development project will be adequately addressed.

Unfortunately, the current fee-to-trust process—as authorized under the Indian Reorganization Act and governed by the Department of the Interior's Part 151 regulations—lacks adequate standards and does not provide any incentive for local governments or tribes to enter into mitigation agreements. The result is a trust land system that gives rise to mutual distrust and dissatisfaction.

We believe that the federal legal framework must be modified to encourage both parties to reach mitigation agreements. This could be done, for example, by establishing a more streamlined fee-to-trust process for cases in which local agreements are in place. Pursuant to CSAC's trust reform proposal, this would be accomplished by exempting a tribe from the need to meet the statutory requirements of subsection (b) if the tribe and the jurisdictional local government(s) have entered into an MOU that address the impacts of the proposed trust acquisition.

In the absence of a mitigation agreement, federal law should require the Secretary to ensure that the interests of the tribe and the jurisdictional local government are balanced in the fee-to-trust process. This should be done by requiring the Secretary to determine, after consulting with appropriate state and local officials, that the proposed land acquisition would not be detrimental to the surrounding community. Additionally, the Secretary should be required to determine that tribes have taken necessary steps to ensure that jurisdictional conflicts and impacts have been mitigated. Once these requirements have been satisfied, the Secretary would be authorized to approve the tribe's development.

Question 2. What should be done if local governments refuse to enter mitigation agreements?

Answer. CSAC does not believe that local governments—or tribes for that matter—should be compelled to enter into mitigation agreements. Indeed, we acknowledge that there will be cases in which neither party will ultimately want to negotiate an MOU no matter how much a potential new fee-to-trust process is able to "incentivize" intergovernmental cooperation.

It is important to note that CSAC's reform proposal would not preclude a tribe from moving forward with a trust application if a local government refuses to enter into an agreement. In such cases, proposed development could move forward as long as other reasonable standards have been met.

While a perfect fee-to-trust process may not be attainable, we remain steadfast in our belief that the best possible system is one that provides a framework for both tribes and local governments to work together.

Question 3. Could you describe the importance of intergovernmental agreements between the tribes and the local governments?

Answer. CSAC believes that intergovernmental agreements between tribes and local governments is essential when one government's development project will significantly impact the other. This cannot be understated given the history of conflict, mistrust, and gridlock that has characterized the current fee-to-trust process.

––––––––

[1] (U.S. Department of the Interior, Office of Inspector General. *Final Evaluation Report on the Process Used to Assess Applications to Take Land into Trust for Gaming Purposes.* Report Number: E–EV–BIA–0063–2003 (2005).

[2] Id., pp. 18.

For the reasons already stated herein, federal statutory law must provide a framework that encourages cooperation between neighboring governments.

Question 4. How should economic self-sufficiency be determined?

Answer. One of the principal goals of Federal Indian policy is to promote tribal economic development and self-sufficiency. Incidentally, the statutes and regulations governing tribes and tribal development do not define self sufficiency or provide further policy guidance relative to how such a standard is to be measured.

In general, economists, think tanks, research centers, and private interest groups agree that economic self-sufficiency is achieved when an individual or family's basic needs—including food, housing, utilities, health care, transportation, taxes, dependent care, clothing, etc.—are consistently met with minimal or no outside financial assistance or subsidies. Expressed as a measurement of income, self-sufficiency is reached when an individual/family has an income of at least 200 percent of the federal poverty level, relative to household size.

CSAC recognizes that the aforementioned measurement, although a widely used standard, may or may not be appropriate for determining whether a tribe and its members have attained economic self-sufficiency. However, since promoting self sufficiency is one of the primary purposes of Federal Indian policy—and in consideration of the significant off-reservation impacts that result from the establishment of casinos and other tribal development projects—we believe that the term, in this context, should be defined in federal law. We therefore urge Congress to carefully consider this issue as part of a broader discussion on fee-to-trust reform, with a particular emphasis on the policy-related implications of potentially applying a different self-sufficiency standard to different socio-economic groups.

Thank you for your leadership on this issue and for your consideration of our views.

————

RESPONSE TO WRITTEN QUESTIONS SUBMITTED BY HON. JOHN BARRASSO TO JACQUELINE JOHNSON-PATA

The fee to trust process involves trust acquisitions of lands located both within an Indian reservation and outside the reservation boundaries. In particular, "off-reservation" trust acquisitions may result in a change of jurisdiction and impact the surrounding community.

Question 1. Please describe some of the ways Indian tribes address jurisdictional issues and mitigate local community impacts for off-reservation trust acquisitions?

Answer. Thank you Senator Barrasso. First, it is important to note that the vast majority of tribal land acquisitions occur in very rural areas, including those that are off-reservation. These are mostly agricultural and forest lands that are adjacent or very near to existing reservations. Most land acquisitions have little impact outside of the tribe.

Of course there are tribes located closer to populated areas, and in these cases there is generally a significant amount of cooperation already in place between the tribal and local government. Most common are public safety and mutual aid agreements. Services agreements and revenue sharing agreements are also common where services are jointly provided. Cooperative land use planning is frequent in populated areas. If new lands are placed into trust, they usually fall under an existing system of tribal and local government cooperation. For the most part, tribes and local governments find that these agreements work very well, services and jurisdiction are seamless, and are capable of providing a higher degree of public services because of the pooling of effort and resources.

Although the clear trend is towards intergovernmental cooperation, of course there are places where relations are strained. Cooperation between tribal and local governments tends to improve when the tribe is a significant part of the local economy. Tribes and local communities have been living and working together for multiple generations, and will continue to do so. Congress should continue to fulfill its trust responsibilities to Indian people by restoring tribal lands and empowering tribes to make positive contributions to the local economy.

Your written testimony submitted for the Committee hearing on November 20, 2013, on "*Carcieri: Bringing Certainty to Trust Land Acquisitions*," states that tribes would never accept a transfer of section 151 authority to state or county governments.

Question 2. What kind of meaningful role can local and county governments have in the section 151 process without transferring authority to them?

Question 2a. Do you believe that the local or county governments' support or opposition to the land into trust acquisition should be taken into consideration by the Secretary?

Answer. I will answer these related questions together. Local and county governments currently play a vital role with their informed participation in the land to trust process, and this option to participate and provide comments is required under the federal regulations at 25 CFR 151. Local government concerns are a critical factor that the Secretary considers regularly. However, in most instances, local concerns are addressed in government-to-government discussions preceding the application to Interior.

The Secretary of Interior is an independent decision maker, confirmed by the Senate, and is charged with making reasonable decisions and weighing the costs and benefits of any land acquisition. In practice, tribes don't waste time on unrealistic plans for discretionary land acquisitions that would transfer significant costs or raise legitimate concerns for the local community. The Secretary's independent and informed decisionmaking role is critical to ensuring that valid local government concerns are properly addressed.

We want to again point out that most issues with county governments relate to off-reservation acquisitions in populated areas, and that the vast majority of acquisitions are much more rural in character. In populated areas it is common that the parties will negotiate conditions and agreements, facilitated by the Secretary's approval function.

Question 3. Do you believe that tribes should be able to state on their application that the land is being taken into trust for one purpose, but then use the land for another purpose without further review by the Bureau of Indian Affairs?

Answer. Existing law prevents tribes or anyone else from making false statements regarding land to trust applications. Interior's land acquisition regulations at Sec. 151.25 state that anyone who knowingly and willfully makes a false statement in connection with a trust title acquisition request may be subject to criminal prosecution under the False Statements Accountability Act of 1996, 18 U.S.C. 1001.

That said, it is entirely possible and even likely that land use plans will change over periods of time, and this is true for every local government in the country. Twenty years ago very few would have predicted the use of land for cell phone towers, now they are ubiquitous across the landscape. Changing land use plans will often cause public debate, but change is inevitable. We do not believe that further federal review is appropriate or necessary for a change in land use plans.

Instead, we should increase cooperation between local and tribal governments on land use planning. This is already common in developed areas, such as the Tulalip Reservation north of Seattle, where cooperative land use planning with Snohomish County has been a foundation for cooperation on economic development, public services, and natural resources protection. Land use planning is much less common in very rural areas, however, for both tribes and local governments.

Land use planning is critical to economic development and improving living conditions for individuals and families in and around Indian Country. Tribal land use planning tends to be siloed on certain programmatic needs—for example transportation or housing. There is a great need for integrated planning across infrastructure needs, and NCAI strongly encourages Congress, as a part of its trust responsibility, to provide additional support for land use planning in Indian country.

Question 4. Do you believe that tribes should be required to mitigate jurisdictional conflicts and effects as a condition for placing land into trust?

Answer. No. As I noted above, there is a great deal more jurisdictional cooperation than conflict in Indian country, and land transfers tend to fall under existing jurisdictional arrangements that have been in place for decades. Of course there are places where cooperation is more difficult, but these are the exception rather than the rule.

In addition, the current process requires the Interior Department to consider all concerns raised by local governments, and the Department's process and independent review heavily favors parties who work together to mitigate impacts.

I should also mention that local communities near Indian reservations already benefit a great deal from federal spending on reservation, from programs such as Johnson O'Malley that provides funds to local schools near reservations, and also from federal Payments in Lieu of Taxes for communities near federal lands.

We urge Congress to keep the context in mind. Restored lands were frequently stolen or unfairly taken from Indian tribes and now tribes must repurchase every square foot before it can be considered for a land to trust transfer. Tribes work very hard to provide services and cooperate with surrounding governments, and the results are impressive. The process should not be held hostage to a mitigation requirement that would be extraordinarily difficult for Interior to manage, would slow the process to a crawl, give even more leverage to local governments, and disadvantage Indian tribes who are the beneficiary of a federal trust responsibility.

In her testimony before the Committee at the hearing on November 20, 2013, on "*Carcieri: Bringing Certainty to Trust Land Acquisitions,*" Senator Feinstein proposed that land taken into trust for non-gaming purposes should be prohibited from being used as casino locations at future dates.

Question 5. Do you agree with this proposal?

Answer. This is already the law for off-reservation acquisitions. Section 20 of the Indian Gaming Regulatory Act prohibits gaming on off-reservation Indian lands acquired in trust after 1988, with only three exceptions:

1.) *Two Part Determinations*—25 USC 2719(b)(1)(A) permits gaming on lands acquired in trust after 1988 if the Secretary of Interior "determines that a gaming establishment on newly acquired lands would be in the best interest of the Indian tribe and its members, and would not be detrimental to the surrounding community, but only if the Governor of the State in which the gaming activity is to be conducted concurs in the Secretary's determination. . ." These acquisitions require wide public engagement on the proposal, and the state's Governor must concur.

2.) *Settlement of Land Claims*—25 USC 2719(b)(1)(B)(i) permits gaming on lands acquired in trust after 1988 if the lands are taken into trust as part of a settlement of a land claim. There are several older settlement statutes that permit certain tribes to select replacement lands in a defined geographic area. These are existing settlements and generally the Secretary lacks discretion in making these acquisitions under federal law. Any acquisitions for gaming purposes require notice to state and local government and public notice and comment under 25 C.F.R. Part 151 and 292.

3.) *Initial Reservation or Restored Lands.* 25 USC 2719(b)(1)(B) permits gaming on lands acquired in trust after 1988 if the lands are taken into trust as part of "(ii) the initial reservation of an Indian tribe acknowledged by the Secretary under the Federal acknowledgment process, or (iii) the restoration of lands for an Indian tribe that is restored to Federal recognition." These acquisitions only occur in a public process where the purpose to acquire the land for gaming purposes is widely shared with state and local governments, and the Department of Interior seeks comment from interested parties under 25 C.F.R. Part 151 and 292.

In her testimony before the Committee at the hearing on November 20, 2013, on "*Carcieri: Bringing Certainty to Trust Land Acquisitions,*" Senator Feinstein noted that casinos require local resources, including increased costs for police, fire, water, sewer, and transportation.

Question 6. Do you believe tribes should be required to mitigate these costs?

Answer. The Indian Gaming Regulatory Act requires tribes and states to negotiate compacts before the tribe can exercise Class III gaming. Compacts may include provisions related to the allocation of criminal and civil jurisdiction and the costs necessary for regulating such activities. Many state governments already receive revenue transfers from tribes for these purposes, and local governments are subdivisions of the states. For example, in Wisconsin the State provides for extensive transfers of gaming revenue funds for local police efforts in cooperation with tribal police. We do not believe it is necessary to provide additional authority to local governments as these issues can and have been resolved through state-tribal compact negotiations. Many tribes provide very substantial contributions to state and local government costs, and these are managed through intergovernmental negotiations.

Question 6a. Please explain how tribes have addressed these costs.

Answer. Most tribes are already providing support for the state budget and for local law enforcement and police departments through gaming compact negotiations.

In addition, many tribes make tangible contributions to assist services in their local area—for example it is remarkable the number of press releases we see where a tribal government has made a contribution in the form of a new fire truck or a police cruiser. Indian tribes are a foundation for economic development in many local areas that is never going to be outsourced to a foreign country, and tribes make enormous contributions in their local communities. In many cases tribes are largest employers in the county and provide jobs and economic support to not only tribal members, but local communities as well.

Question 7. Have there been any instances where disputes arose between tribes and local, county, or state governments regarding mitigating, paying for, or entering agreements to address these local impacts?

Answer. Of course local debates arise from time to time about revenue and services—which are the primary topics of every government discussion. For example, until recently some of the tribes in New York were withholding payment until the terms of their compacts were fulfilled. But the State of New York and the tribes engaged in a series of far-reaching settlements that will benefit both the tribes and their neighbors. We urge Congress to continue to trust in the good will and track record of government-to-government negotiations. Cooperation between tribal and local governments tends to improve when the tribe is empowered, and is making positive contributions to the local economy and governmental services. Congress should continue to fulfill its trust responsibilities to Indian people, restore tribal lands, and empower tribes to make positive contributions to the local economy and governmental services.

In her written testimony submitted for the Committee hearing on November 20, 2013, on "*Carcieri: Bringing Certainty to Trust Land Acquisitions,*" Ms. Diane Dillon recommended several changes to the land into trust process. One recommendation is that trust land requests cannot be approved when negative impacts to other parties outweigh the benefit to the tribe.

Question 8. What do you think about balancing these impacts and benefits?

Answer. As I mentioned above, the Secretary of Interior is a Senate-confirmed cabinet member who is charged with exercising discretion to make these judgments. Tribes work very hard to provide services and cooperate with surrounding governments, and the results are impressive. We do not believe it would be appropriate to create a mitigation requirement that would be extraordinarily difficult for Interior to quantify or apply, would slow the process to a crawl, give even more leverage to local governments, and disadvantage Indian tribes who are the beneficiary of a federal trust responsibility.

————

RESPONSE TO WRITTEN QUESTIONS SUBMITTED BY HON. JOHN BARRASSO TO HON. MARSHALL PIERITE

In her written testimony submitted for the Committee hearing on November 20, 2013, on "*Carcieri: Bringing Certainty to Trust Land Acquisitions,*" Ms. Diane Dillon recommended several changes to the land into trust process. One recommendation is that trust land requests cannot be approved when negative impacts to other parties outweigh the benefit to the tribe.

Question 1. What do you think about balancing these impacts and benefits?

Answer. This question must be considered within the historical context of broken promises and illegal dispossession of tribes from their land. Although we should strive to find justice and balance, a part of the equation must include a recognition that tribes had their land stolen from them and now are forced to buy it back.

Question 2. Could you describe some of the impacts that *Carcieri* has had on Indian tribes?

Answer. Tribes are working every day to improve the welfare of their people through projects for community and economic development. The uncertainty over the status of their land has increased risk to potential investors which has led in many cases to an increase in the cost of capital for projects, and the inability to find capital for others. The *Carcieri* decision has stagnated job growth and diminished the chance for thousands of people to increase their standard of living and provide a more certain future for their children.

Question 3. How important do you think it is for tribes to work with local governments when taking land into trust that is not contingent to an existing Indian reservation?

Answer. Tribes work on a daily basis with their local non-Indian neighbors. While many people would like to spread fear in those places where tribes are seeking to develop new economic development facilities, the truth is that tribal enterprises are a positive force in local communities and in most cases a strong mutually beneficial relationship evolves. We encourage all tribes to seek strong partnerships with local governments, but we cannot agree that local governments should have a veto power over projects on tribal land—land that was in most cases stolen from the tribe to begin with.

Response to the following written questions was not received before the hearing's print deadline

WRITTEN QUESTIONS SUBMITTED TO HON. KEVIN WASHBURN

The written testimony from Ms. Diane Dillon submitted for the Committee hearing on November 20, 2013, on "*Carcieri: Bringing Certainty to Trust Land Acquisitions*," states that the acceptance rate for section 151 fee-to-trust applications from the Bureau of Indian Affairs (BIA) Pacific Regional Office was 100 percent from 2001 to 2011.

Question. How many section 151 applications were received, withdrawn, accepted, and denied in that Office in the past 10 years?

Question. How many section 151 applications have been received, withdrawn, accepted, and denied in all BIA regions in the past 10 years?

Your written testimony submitted for the Committee hearing on November 20, 2013, on "*Carcieri: Bringing Certainty to Trust Land Acquisitions*," questions whether tribes should be asked at all what their purpose for taking land into trust is.

Question. Do you question this provision as well for off-reservation acquisitions?

Question. How would local communities and governments provide meaningful comments on a tribal application when the purpose is unknown?

In her written testimony submitted for the Committee hearing on November 20, 2013, on "*Carcieri: Bringing Certainty to Trust Land Acquisitions*," Ms. Diane Dillon states that the state, county, and local governments are only afforded limited notice and consultation on pending applications.

Question. Please describe in detail the process of notifying state, county, and local governments and of receiving comments from local governments and local communities (i.e., do you conduct town hall meetings or consultation, etc., if so, how are they conducted).

Question. Please describe how the input of these governments and communities affects the decision on whether the land is taken into trust.

Question. Do intergovernmental agreements help streamline the fee-to-trust process?

Question. Do you believe there is something that should be done to expedite land-into-trust applications that are accompanied by an intergovernmental agreement?

According to data received from the Bureau of Indian Affairs (BIA) regarding land-into-trust acquisitions, there have been 18 applications for land into trust accepted over the last 4 years, for which the purpose of the acquisition is "unidentified." The data received from the BIA also states that only 13 of the land-into-trust applications were for gaming.

Question. How can the Secretary evaluate the application and conduct an environmental assessment or impact statement when no purpose is provided in the fee to trust application?

Question. What kind of BIA oversight exists to ensure the current and future uses of the trust land are consistent with the purpose for which the land was taken into trust?

Question. What happens if the purpose that the land was taken into trust for is not the purpose being carried out on the land?

In her testimony before the Committee hearing on November 20, 2013, on "*Carcieri: Bringing Certainty to Trust Land Acquisitions*," Senator Feinstein proposes that land taken into trust for non-gaming purposes should be prohibited from being used as casino locations at future dates.

Question. Do you agree with this proposal?

In her written testimony submitted for the Committee hearing on November 20, 2013, on "*Carcieri: Bringing Certainty to Trust Land Acquisitions*," Ms. Diane Dillon proposed that land be taken into trust on the condition that it is used for the intended purpose. She further proposes that if the purpose is changed, the land into trust application must be further reviewed.

Question. Do you agree with this proposal?

On November 13, 2013, the Administration published a final rule amending the land acquisition regulations in 25 CFR Part 151. Ms. Diane Dillon's written testimony submitted for the Committee hearing on November 20, 2013, on "*Carcieri: Bringing Certainty to Trust Land Acquisitions*," states that this new rule will allow tribes to immediately begin development of the trust land and result in irreparable damage to local governments even if the local governments receive a favorable decision in court.

Question. Could you describe how this rule mitigates the impacts of the Patchak decision?

Question. How would the BIA manage or treat lands that had been taken into trust but, after the acquisition, a court holds that the acquisition was outside the scope of the Secretary's authority and that the acquisition was invalid?

Question. How would this invalidation of a Secretarial acquisition affect the application of the final rule published on November 13, 2013 to the acquisition or other trust land applications?

Data received from the Bureau of Indian Affairs indicates that only 13 applications for land-into-trust for gaming purposes have been approved in the past 4 years.

Question. How many have been submitted in that timeframe?